Diogo da Annunciação Justiniano, Carlos Vero, Moses Mocatta

The Inquisition and Judaism 1705

A sermon addressed to Jewish martyrs

Diogo da Annunciação Justiniano, Carlos Vero, Moses Mocatta

The Inquisition and Judaism 1705
A sermon addressed to Jewish martyrs

ISBN/EAN: 9783337147310

Printed in Europe, USA, Canada, Australia, Japan

Cover: Foto ©Lupo / pixelio.de

More available books at **www.hansebooks.com**

THE INQUISITION AND JUDAISM.

A SERMON

ADDRESSED TO

JEWISH MARTYRS,

ON THE OCCASION OF AN AUTO DA FE AT LISBON, 1705.

BY

THE ARCHBISHOP OF CRANGANOR;

ALSO

A REPLY TO THE SERMON,

BY

CARLOS VERO.

TRANSLATED BY

MOSES MOCATTA.

PHILADELPHIA:
BARNARD & JONES, PRINTERS, RIDGWAY BUILDINGS.
No. 510 Minor Street.
5620.

NOTE.

We think that we render a service to the cause of Judaism by reprinting this controversial work which we received some years ago from the late Moses Mocatta, and which he had translated from the Portuguese. Mr. M. printed all his works for private distribution, and this one has, therefore, like the others, never been accessible to the public.

We would observe, that Mr. M. belonged to the British Jews' congregation who do not regard rabbinical authority as binding. Hence his allusion in the Preface which is not very complimentary to our old teachers.

Should the sale of this tract be such as to demonstrate that such books will be acceptable to a large class of readers, we may then be induced to issue some others which ought to become more generally diffused.   I. L.

Philadelphia, August, 5620.

INTRODUCTION.

In the following pages will be found a sermon delivered by the Archbishop of Cranganor to a number of Israelites, hapless victims of the Inquisition, preparatory to the unhallowed celebration of an auto da fé. Of the unfortunate beings compelled to listen to the archbishop, a majority were under sentence of making their selection between apostacy and death, and one amongst the number, having offended a second time against the Inquisition, is, agreeably to all inference, irrevocably condemned to perish by the flames. And yet it is before such defenceless creatures, whose tongues are bridled, that the prelate effects a vast display of erudition; it is such unhappy men whom he assails with a verbose and diffuse harangue, professing to enter into a *free* and *fair* discussion on the merits of the respective creeds of Judaism and Christianity!

Such a flagrant outrage on the unalienable rights of conscience—such a solemn farce, enacted in the name and under the assumed sanction of the God of mercy and love—cannot fail to awaken in every humane and thinking mind sentiments of abhorrence and disgust. Painful as the records of such acts must be, still we may derive a soothing consolation from the fact that the Satanic tribunal of Torquemado, every page of whose history is inscribed in blood, has long ceased to be tolerated by every civilized nation throughout the globe. Though the times in which our lives are cast bear the impress of a more humane and enlightened spirit, and render impracticable the barbarous deeds of the mediæval ages; we have nevertheless to deplore that the privileges of conscience are not yet respected, and that the morbid craving for apostatizing still continues to mar domestic and social peace, and to keep alive the flame of civil and sectarian strife which ought long since to have been extinguished.

In many parts of the Old and New World, but more especially in Great Britain, the conversion of the Jews has become an organized system.— Here, societies and branch societies are formed, schools are established for infants and adults, and enormous sums are annually placed at the disposal of mercenary agents to further what the maudlin fanaticism of the day calls "the good cause." It might be imagined that with all this formidable apparatus, added to the efforts of a regiment of missionaries in no way scrupulous as to the means they employ to accomplish their unrighteous object, that every year would bring an overwhelming number of Jews to the baptismal font. Nothing, however, can be more contrary to the fact; for if we are to give credence to the printed reports of the conversionists (and most anxious must they be to make some show in return for the treasure poured into their coffers), eighteen, or, at most, nineteen is the yearly average of Jewish souls that can be brought up for the society in the several districts of their missionary stations.

On inquiring into the true motives that can possibly induce Israelites to renounce the faith of their fathers, we cannot divest ourselves of the suspicion that a craving for mundane honors, and an unruly ambition upon which religious sentiment holds no check, may have great weight with some men, and may lead them to prefer the momentary gratification which the parade and circumstance of power confers, to the favor of the Supreme Being and the approbation of conscience. To attempt to argue with such unprincipled men, if such there be, would be utterly hopeless; for little can the words of mortals avail who are deaf to the voice of God and reckless of their eternal bliss.

Others, again, there are, whose abject poverty renders them obnoxious to the pecuniary bait held out by the wily agents of the "Society."— We are hardly prepared to suggest a remedy in this case, indisposed as we are to attempt to bind men to their creed by mere worldly considerations: yet would we venture to urge on the consideration of the more opulent members of our community the absolute necessity of taking a deep and lively interest in the condition of their poorer brethren, of ascertaining their mental and physical wants, and of endeavoring to protect them, as far as may be practicable, from the demoralizing influence of those who traffic in conscience.

There is, however, another class of Israelites, neither few nor unimportant, who are deserving of the highest consideration. We allude to the youths of both sexes, who, for want of that sound religious instruction which the pulpit of every Synagogue ought to provide, but which at the present day is almost entirely neglected, are left to their own resources, and are thus rendered an easy prey to whoever may be disposed to steal away their hearts. Every one conversant with the religious training of Jewish females must be impressed with the lamentable fact that the instruction imparted to this important class of the community is fatally deficient. To them the Scriptures in the orignal Hebrew are as a sealed book: their sole dependance is on the authorized Anglican version, which every Hebraist must be aware, is an extremely partial translation, often at war with the obvious grammatical sense of the verse and of the context, and avowedly, or at least designedly, undertaken to give a coloring to a system unknown to Moses and to the succeeding prophets, and therefore subversive of the teachings of the genuine Hebrew Scriptures. These unfair and perverted translations, added to the objectionable and totally unwarranted headings of the chapters, often perplex readers of tender years, and fill their minds with misgivings and doubts. Confiding in what they suppose to be a faithful, accurate, and conscientious rendering of the Old Testament, and receiving little or no aid from their own clergy as to the proper exposition of the Scriptures, they either regard the Bible as involving manifest contradictions, and so degenerate into infidelity, or they fall into the snares spread for their feet by the mercenary agents of the converting societies. It is for this class, and principally for the female portion of this class, the future wives and mothers in Israel, who must naturally form the religious principles of the coming generation, that the translator of the sermon of the archbishop and of its refutation, has imposed on himself the present task.

Whoever has noted the history of the controversy between the "Converters" and the disciples of the faith of Moses, must be aware that the weapons employed have been invariably taken from the same armory. The reader will not, therefore, be surprised at the want of novelty in the "proofs" and "arguments" advanced by the "converters," from the prelate of Cranganor downwards; but he will be rejoiced to find that the able reply of the Israelites (whom either a high sense of modesty or more probably, a fear of persecution, has induced to conceal his name), strikes at the root of all the positions taken up by the champion of Papacy, and proves each of his arguments to be inconsequent and unscriptural. Every book of the Bible, and every volume recording the opinions of individual Rabbins, has been ransacked by the coercing baptisers during a succession of centuries, and yet they have found no sharper weapons wherewith to combat the pure principles of Mosaism than those employed by the Archbishop of Cranganor.

The reply, therefore, to the prelate of Lisbon, is a reply to the whole of his fraternity who have since embarked in the same unjustifiable warfare. Let, then, the discerning reader make himself familiar with the sentiments and doctrines of both disputants: let him study the sermon and the reply: let him "look on this picture and on that;" then let him compare the Jesuitical sophistry of the former with the unimpassioned logic of the latter; and it may reasonably be anticipated that he will cling with increased fondness and confidence to the faith of his fathers, and that he will live and die a disciple of Moses, not only from the circumstance of birth, habit, and early associations, but from absolute conviction induced by the native force of truth.

The old and somewhat curious work now put forth, having made its way, by mere chance, to the translator, he at once deemed it a religious duty to give it an English attire, and to secure for it a ready reception amongst the youthful portion of his Jewish brethren, by presenting it to them *gratis*. It is to be regretted that some steps in the same direction have not long since been taken by those whose bounden duty it is to train youth in religious knowledge. For better would it have been for the moral and spiritual welfare of Israel, if the Rabbins of other times had manifested less concern for every tittle of outward ceremonies, and had displayed more earnestness for the development of the exalted principles which constitute the basis and the glory of the Jewish faith. Had they but imitated the example of the מתורגמן* in the days of Ezra, had they stood forth like him to expound the law in the vernacular tongue, instead of spending their lives in subtle speculations, and in fine hair drawn disquisitions which exercise no moral or religious influence over the minds of youth, how many would, even at the present day, be worshipping the God of Israel as an absolute Unity, instead of bowing at the shrine of apostacy.

The translator has frankly avowed his object

---

* The Chaldee for interpreter.

in introducing the following work to the notice of the youth of Israel—that it is intended to fortify them in the principles of their ancient faith, and to protect them against the insidious efforts of the missionaries. To this faithful declaration he begs to add, that nothing is more remote from his mind and more alien to his wishes than to interfere with the religious belief of his Christian brethren and compatriots. A genuine Israelite is, both from doctrine and feeling, an uncompromising friend to freedom of conscience.—Whilst he is naturally attached to his own faith, it is with him a practical doctrine that all men of all creeds, whose lives are morally good, are equally the objects of the Almighty's love and care, and that they will all participate in the blessings of life everlasting. Far then from condemning the creeds of other men, the Israelite respects all religious systems, however they may differ from his own, and regards them as the several means by which men are rendered useful, happy, and morally good; and by which they are brought nearer and nearer to that Great Being, "the Rock, whose work is perfection."*

Never, therefore, will the Israelites be found attacking the faith of another; but if he is compelled to enter the lists of controversy, it is on the side of the defence that his banner will be

---

* Deut. xxxii. 4.

unfurled, and there he will be seen verifying the impressive scriptural axiom:—דבר בעתו מה טוב "a word in season, how good is it!" In an admirable little work just issued from the press, we notice the following acute and judicious remark:* "So long as the Christian confines his arguments and quotations to the New Testament, the Israelite feels perfectly secure, from his entire rejection of such authority as divine: but when the words of the Old Testament are so explained as to bear most startlingly upon the creed of our adversaries, then it is that we need a careful but perfectly simple training to supply us with reply and defence." It is to be hoped that the work now placed in the hands of Jewish youths, will supply the desideratum to which the authoress refers.

The writer of the refutation has merely confined himself to the compass of the Archbishop of Cranganor's arguments; and the scriptural quotations which he has adduced in support are consequently narrowed to that prescribed limit. Let it not, therefore, be imagined that all the proofs which the Bible can furnish in defence of Judaism, are exhausted in this reply; far from it, since there is scarcely a chapter of the book of Deuteronomy, nor a book of the prophets, which the writer might not have quoted in support of his defence, had it been necessary to his purpose.

---

*Women of Israel, by Grace Aguilar.

B

The reader may, however, repose unlimited confidence in all the expositions and elucidations which the writer of the "Reply" has put forth. The translator, who, during more than half a century of a prolonged life devoted to the study of the genuine Hebrew Scriptures, and to every controversial work of note from the pen of Jews and Christians, has carefully examined and verified all the quotations employed by the writer of the "Reply," and has found them to be fully trustworthy. He is devoutly thankful to Almighty God for having vouchsafed to him the time and the opportunity to make himself thoroughly acquainted with the idiom of the original text, so that his heart is indelibly impressed with the sublime and immortal truths of Judaism.

The translator would fain offer a word or two, as to the *manner* in which he has endeavored to perform his task. In order to render impartial justice to both disputants, he has felt it right even at the sacrifice of elegance of style and propriety of expression, to give a faithful literal version both of the *Portuguese* homily and the *Spanish* reply. To do this he has ventured to retain all the prolixity and tautology of the "Sermon," as well as much of the quaintness and unevenness of style which give a harshness to both compositions. If these be considered blemishes, the judicious reader will attribute them less to the writers themselves than to the age in which they flourished.

The task of the translator is now at an end: he has only to offer this work to the favorable and attentive consideration of his readers, and to entreat them to make themselves familiar with the Scriptures in the original Hebrew, which knowledge will prove to them a valuable blessing; finally, he conjures every son and daughter of Israel to regard as the Cynosure that is to guide them through life, the emphatic exhortation of Scripture:—

אתה הראת לדעת כי יי הוא האלהים אין עוד מלבדו

"Unto thee it was shown that thou mightest be convinced that the Eternal He is God, there is none besides Him." (Deut. iv. 35.)   M. M.

SERMON

OF

THE AUTO DA FE.

CELEBRATED IN THE PUBLIC SQUARE IN THE CITY OF LISBON, NEAR THE OFFICE OF THE INQUISITION, ON THE 6TH SEPTEMBER, 1705, IN THE PRESENCE OF THEIR HIGHNESSES.

PREACHED BY

THE MOST ILLUSTRIOUS AND MOST REVEREND

SENHOR DON DIEGO ANNUNCIAZARO JUSTINIANO,

ONE OF THE COUNCIL OF HIS MAJESTY (WHOM GOD PRESERVE), AND LATE ARCHBISHOP OF CRANGANOR.

SERMON AT AN AUTO DA FE,

ETC.

"*Ipse autem populus direptus et vastatus; laqueus juvenum omnes, et in domibus carcerum absconditi sunt; facti sunt in rapinum, nec est qui eruat; in direptionem, nec est qui dicat: Redde.*"

Isaiah, cap. xlii. 22.

Most High and Mighty Prince, and Lords.

I.

OH! degraded remnants of Judaism, unhappy fragments of the Synagogue! the last spoil of Judea! opprobrium of the Catholics! abhorrence and laughing-stock of your fellow Jews, it is to you I address myself, ye misguided men! You are the abhorrence and laughing-stock of the Jews; for your ignorance is such that you know not how to observe the very law you profess.— You are the opprobrium of the Catholics; for, being born within the pale of its church, your voluntary apostacy has banished you from its bosom; you are the last spoil of Judea, for, (to our shame,) your lot is cast here in Portugal to disgrace and scandalize us in the opinion of the whole world—in our quarter of the globe as well as in your native East. You are the wretched fragments of Synagogue, for all its former greatness is come to an end in your present misery. Finally, you are a degraded remnant of Judaism, the wretched offshoots of Israel, who, since the destruction of your country, have spread throughout Europe to infect whole nations by your presence.

II.

You are a people whose patience has never been exhausted by long-protracted hope, to whose minds the clearest evidence does not bring conviction, whom the severest suffering only disposes the more inveterately to persist in your obstinacy. Chastisement that softens brutes, only makes you more stubborn. Evidence that convinces even fools, only renders you more positive. Hope that wearies the spirit of others, makes you more enduring. You have, from the first, been deceived by four dotards, who have taught you to expect the Messiah after Christ had come into the world; so that instead of your hopes being abandoned upon that event, they have encouraged you to persevere in them, and to cling with desperation to your faith.

III.

How greatly do I pity your degradation, O children of Israel! how many tears of blood I shed through compassion for your misfortunes, contemplating what you are at this day, and what you formerly were. In ancient times, the inheritors of that affection which your continued obstinacy did not deserve; this day the objects of well-merited anger, which fulfils in you, a just retribution; this day the scaffold is the theatre of your contumely; formerly, your tabernacles were the boast of your religion. In ancient times, the waters held you in respect, and no less the flames; this day fire will feed on you, and your ashes, cast into the sea, will find a tomb in the waters. Now, everybody shuns your society; anciently, everybody courted your friendship. Anciently, trumpets sounded the glory you reaped from the observance of your law; this day trumpets proclaim your infamy in the superstitious observance (I will not say of an expiring law, but) of a law actually extinct. At the present time, to be a Jew is considered a reproach in every country; formerly, to be a Jew was deemed an honor throughout the world; formerly, your tents in the desert were dwellings wherein Heaven showered upon you its favors; now, your depopulated habitations are dwellings wherein the fire of justice reduces you to ashes. This day, the anniversary of your feast of Purim, is the day when you are to abjure and make atonement for your sins in the yellow and scarlet colors of your penitential dresses—the emblems of the fire which will consume your dwelling-places, unless these dresses be changed for another color before being committed to the flames. In former times, on the day of atonement for your sins, the scarlet thread that was bound on the horns of the goat which was to be sacrificed on that day was changed into white, to show that God had pardoned your sins. In former times, your inheritance was the unalienable property of your families; now, the public treasury is your heir.

It is more than sixteen hundred and thirty-two years since Titus brought destruction upon you; yet are you still lingering in bondage, and God only knows when your captivity will come to an end. Formerly, your God was so disposed to have mercy on your sufferings that your troubles never lasted more that a few years. Thus, on account of selling Joseph into bondage, which was your first sin, and in which all your progenitors conspired, you were punished by a pilgrimage in Egypt during the limited period of ninety-one years. In the time of the Judges, the dispersion you underwent for your idolatries, which formed your second crime, and in which your ancestors were all implicated, ended in a hundred and eleven years. In Babylon, whither you were banished for having murdered your prophets, your captivity ended in about seventy years. Such was the extent of your punishment when you put your prophets to death, worshipped idols, and sold the innocent.

IV.

Truly, O children, dear to my soul! the condition in which you are at the present day compared with what you were in times past, would soften a heart far less obdurate than mine; for though we may not be of the same blood, we are all your brethren through the blood of Jesus Christ who redeemed you, and through the holy water of baptism, wherewith you have been sprinkled.

Truly, O unhappy race! this change should in itself be sufficient to convert fools: how much more so you who boast of possessing knowledge? The contemplation of what you once were and what you now are, should serve to convert you from what you are to what you ought to be; and if it should please the God of Israel, our God as well as yours, to cause you to repent this day with all your heart, it is in your power, by making abjuration, to give authentic evidence of the sincerity of your conversion. Without giving you offence—for my wish is solely to convince you—I shall endeavor to show you your error, and so undeceive you with regard to your tenets, so that, if you are reasonable beings, you cannot fail to become Catholics. Unhappy men! who, ignorant of the very creed you profess, mistake ridiculous forms for acts of religion, how I could wish that all your teachers, who are scattered over the world, could be here this day to be my hearers; for so demonstratively shall I destroy the foundation of your hopes, that you would be compelled, by their judgment as well as your own, to become of the number of the faithful, however obstinately you and they might wish to persist in remaining Jews. True it is, that without a pious disposition of the will, it is hard to convince the understanding: still, so forcible are the arguments that I shall this day submit to your attention, that they cannot fail to elicit from your judgment a conclusion adverse to the falsehood of yours, and in favor of the truth of our faith.

V.

In order that the demonstrations I may give may prove of sufficient efficacy to convince you of your error, I shall not advance any theological arguments; for these depend on principles which either are unknown to you through ignorance, or will be rejected by your stubborn apostacy. I will not avail myself of the New Testament; for your creed will not admit the supposition, that through baptism you are constrained to believe in its truth; neither will I attempt to persuade you by the evidence of our fathers, as I suppose their authority will be held in suspicion by your incredulous minds; nor by the rendering of the Old Testament according to our vulgate, as you do not admit that to be canonical; but by your own Hebrew or Chaldaic version, which you hold as sacred authority, not admitting of doubt or controversy. This, then, will be the text from which I shall draw all my arguments. The expositions of your Rabbins, on whose doctrines you ground your faith as Jews, will be added in corroboration. Only listen dispassionately to me, and you will find that prejudice must yield to the force of evidence.

VI.

The prophet Isaiah, in chapter xlii. of his prophecies, saw in a vision the wretched state into which the Jews, on account of their sins, would fall after the advent of Christ, who was and is the true Messiah which God promised to the world in his Scriptures, and left them a warning against their delusion in these words: "*Ipse autem populus direptus et vastatus; laqueus juvenum omnes, et in domibus carcerum absconditi sunt; facti sunt in rapinam, nec est qui eruat; in direptionem, nec est qui dicat: Redde.*"

Know, ye unhappy people (says the prophet), know that after the coming of the Messiah, you will be a dispetsed nation throughout the world, and bondsmen in every land; for you are to be a ruided and scattered people: "*Ipse autem populus direptus et vastatus.*"

The small remnants of your former greatness, which are left as an authentic testimony of the chastisement of your sins, shall form a net that

c

will, with a sudden motion, draw you into a fearful prison, so that each shall be taken into a separate dungeon and immured in his cell with such secrecy that no one shall know who went in yesterday, and the one who is taken there to-day shall not know who it is that goes in to-morrow: *"In domibus carcerum absconditi sunt."*

You will be reduced to such misery, O unfortunate people! that your nation of young and old will be quarrelling with one another; and you will form a net for your mutual distress and entanglement: *"Laqueus juvenum universitas ipsorum vel omnes ipsi,"* says your Hebrew text.

Thus conformably to the prophecy, you confound and entangle yourselves, O wretched sons of Israel, whom a severe imprisonment awaits, which you have no means of averting; for Judaism being the crime with which you are charged, your involvement is such that no aid can avail to affect your liberation: *"Facti sunt in rapinam, nec est qui eruat; in direptionem, nec est qui dicat: Redde."*

VII.

That this passage in Isaiah contemplated the punishment that the Jews are now suffering, your own experience must be sufficient to convince you; for you yourselves are in the very condition into which the prophet says you would fall after the advent of the Messiah. You yourselves see how you are dispersed all over the world, and scattered throughout every land; and either from necessity or inclination hold yourselves apart from one another, so that even if you meet privately to perform the rights of Judaism, you avoid each other in public, in order to deceive those who charge you with being Jews. You yourselves bewail your misfortunes, and complain to us Catholics that your enemies ensnare you, and draw you so suddenly and indiscriminately into the meshes of our holy office, that all of your lineage are exposed to the same calamity; and although you mutually proclaim your afflictions to one another, there is no one who has the power to rescue you therefrom. All these facts, founded upon your own experience, fully prove that the prophet alludes to you in his text. If it be possible to suppose that this argument is not sufficient to establish the point, the evidence of your own Rabbi Samuel will serve to do so; for a thousand years ago, this Rabbi, in his celebrated epistle, acknowledges that Rabbi Isaac, seven hundred and five years previously, had written that this captivity had befallen you for the sin you committed in putting Christ to death: *"Apertè dicit Deus quod erit desolatio post occisionem Christi; sicut est nostra desolatio, postquam Jesus fuit occisus."*

VIII.

My brethren, do you see all these tokens already fulfilled, of what was to happen to you after the Messiah had come, according to the word of your prophet? Either you do or you do not. If you do not, you are blind; for the very thing is at this moment happening to every individual among you. If you do, why do you not disabuse yourselves, and admit that your hope is a manifest error, and that the Messiah you expect can never come, since these tokens prove that he has already been? Subsequently to the Messiah's coming, you were to be a dispersed and ruined people: *"Populus direptus et vastatus."* You were all to be ensnared conjointly or separately: *"Laqueus universitas ipsorum, vel omnes ipsi."*— You were not to be imprisoned together in gaol, but each of you was to have a separate cell to himself: *"In domibus carcerum absconditi sunt."*— So strong was to be the prison, and so rigid the confinement, that no arm would be able to rescue you therefrom: *"Facti sunt in rapinam, nec est qui eruat; in direptionem, nec est qui dicat: Redde."*

Now, at this day, if you experience all these things, and your ancestors have experienced the same for so many years past, how can you expect a future advent, if it was after the advent all these things were to occur? What madness in you to look to the future for what is already past! After witnessing the consequences that were to follow the advent of the Messiah, you still continue to look forward to that event. The captivity continues, the imprisonment does not cease, the net goes on strengthening, the dispersion extending, the destruction is prolonged, and the Messiah does not appear. After the Messiah had come, you were to undergo all this: the event proves that the coming has already taken place; and yet you, with this event in view, still expect him to come. Verily, this is a part of the severe punishment that God has inflicted on you for the horrid sacrilege of murdering his son.—You hope for the Messiah in opposition to the very reasons of that for which you hope; and thus, although no longer in a position to expect him, inasmuch as he has already appeared, you persist, like desperate men, in hoping against all hope. God promised you a Messiah who was to come, and who accordingly came; you, in your despair on seeing that he has come, obstinately continue to hope for a future Messiah, who, it is impossible, in the nature of things, can come, and yet, in spite of this absolute impossibility, persist in hoping for him, because you cannot bring yourselves to lay such hopes altogether aside. According to the most approved chronology, since the time of Abraham, when God more explicitly promised you the Messiah, you have had three thousand six hundred and fifteen years of hope, and you are not yet tired; for you still go on hoping, and will continue to do so until the end of the world. Courageous must be the Jewish mind, that can thus hope on untiringly.

c*

Cruel Messiah, who has so long delayed and will so long delay to appear! O enduring people, that can still so perseveringly wait for the Messiah! But hope as much as you please, you may undeceive yourselves; for so long as you will not have done with your hopes, and confess that beside the person of Jesus Christ no other Messiah is possible, your redemption will not take place, your captivity will continue, and your chastisement be prolonged.

IX.

"*Nec est qui eruat; nec est qui dicat: Redde.*"— Now upon the face of it, this passage of Isaiah evidently implies, that it is to be understood as relating to the Jews and the punishment which they were to undergo in their final dispersion. For the prophet affirms that the Jews will not have a redeemer till they are freed from their present captivity; and if any one of us ask you how long your captivity is to endure, you can only reply, that so long as the Messiah whom you expect does not come, you will continue to undergo your present sufferings. So that if the Jews place their hope of redemption in a future Messiah (and they are still expecting the Messiah), why does the prophet say that they are not to have redemption? For the precise reason that the Jews expect their redemption from a future Messiah, they must remain without relief; for no new Messiah will ever be sent to them; and as such a Messiah is impossible, so is the relief impossible that the Jews expect therefrom.

X.

The Messiah the Jews expect is impossible, from the very nature of the predictions which the Jews persuade themselves that the Messiah has to satisfy. It is impossible, from the time in which he was to come, and also from the signs having been already verified in Christ, which cannot be again fulfilled in any other.

It is impossible, from the time in which he is to appear; for the time was already past when Christ came, and it is impossible that a time which is past can return again. It is, moreover, impossible from the nature of the predictions which the Jews persuade themselves that the Messiah has to satisfy, since these very predictions prove, that in the Messiah they have been already fulfilled; and, considering this impossibility, the Messiah whom the Jews expect is no other than a mere chimera which their obstinacy has invented. The prophet, in order to convince the Jews that their hope was a fable, and the object of their desire but a dream, told them, that the more they hoped, the longer it would be before they obtained the object of their hope, and the accomplishment of their wishes: *"Nec est qui eruat; nec est qui dicat: Redde."*

XI.

I shall next proceed to prove that the hope of the Jews is self-destructive, for that they are expecting a Messiah whom they ought not, inasmuch as, on every rational principle, a Messiah such as the Jews expect is an impossibility. The conclusion must be apparent to those who are sincere in their desire to embrace the truth, as they will be unable to resist the force of the evidence which I shall adduce. I might well be discouraged and disheartened by the hopelessness of reaping any fruit from my labors, seeing how inadequate my arguments must be to destroy your stubbornness, when Christ with his miracles could not vanquish the obstinacy of your predecessors. But surely the human understanding cannot for ever resist the force of truth, however unfavorable the inclination may be to its reception. I will address myself to your judgment and not to your will; I say, not to your will, because words cannot conquer obstinate determination; but rather to your judgment, because the understanding must give assent to truth. Only attend to me with a pious affection of the will, without previous obduracy of heart, and your judgment cannot fail to be so convinced as to cause you to abjure sincerely your error, and renounce your opposition. We will now enter upon the discussion, and begin by adducing the particulars that were predicted concerning the Messiah.

XII.

In order to prove to you the impossibility of the Messiah whom you expect, by the actual predictions from which you infer what the Messiah is to be when he comes, and to make apparent to you the fallacy of your expectations, it is requisite to ask you whether you expect a Messiah such as God had promised to you through His prophets, or whether you expect one fashioned after the fancy of a few ignorant men, who, deceiving themselves and you, have invented an absurd Messiah, and presented him as the true one to your credulity?

If your expectations were of the first kind, your hope would be just, supposing that the Messiah had not already sanctified the world with his presence. If your expectations are of the latter kind, you are mad; inasmuch as you set in opposition to God's truth the idle story of a few idiots, who seek to amuse you with delusive hopes. As men of sense, I know you will answer me, that the Messiah, whenever he should appear, would be such as God revealed through His prophets. Tell me now what is to be the Messiah whom you expect? Is he to be a mere man like Moses, who delivered you from Egyptian captivity, or like Zerubbabel, who redeemed you from the Babylonian bondage? I well know that you, or your teachers for you, will answer me that the Messiah will possess far higher attributes, as he will deliver you from your present oppression, and restore you to a more glorious freedom. The same all your Rabbins affirm in their Talmud, see *Sanhedrin*, chap. *Helek*.

XIII.

Again I ask you, The Messiah whom you still expect, presuming him more powerful than Zerubbabel or Moses, is he to be a mere man as these two were, or will he be man and God, as these two were not? On the reply to this depends the truth of our faith and the falsity of yours. A modern sect among your Rabbins advises you to give no reply to this question (and they do well, for your reply would infallibly enable us to convince you of your error), and to this end they persuade you that when you cannot get excused from making a reply, you should deny the point of a Messiah altogether, saying that he never came, nor ever will come, for that the advent of the Messiah is not an article of your faith, and that Judaism does not consist in that expectation, but in the true observance of the law of Moses, which is the only thing obligatory on the Jews.

XIV.

To understand correctly this point, it is requisite to know that, with regard to the Messiah, the Jews of the present day are divided into two entirely different and opposite opinions. Some say, and that is the general opinion among your wretched people, that the Messiah has not yet come. Others assert that he came one thousand six hundred and thirty-two years ago, having been born at the period when Titus destroyed Jerusalem. So it is written in the Talmud in *Beresheet Raba* (which is in substance a copious commentary upon Genesis) chap. *Echa*. Also in the book *Sanhedrin* in the chapter *Cum similiter*. And as it is maintained, according to this opinion, that the Messiah has already come, no less than one thousand six hundred and thirty-two years must have elapsed since his advent; and yet, during all that time, no Jew has seen him. Some even say that he is still wandering unknown about the world; others, that he stands at the gates of Rome in company with the poor, soliciting alms; others, that he is concealed in the Caspian hills, with such precautions, that if an attempt should be made to go in search of him, the river Sabbatine would present an invincible obstruction; for on any Jew's approaching its margin, its waters are suddenly petrified, and rain down so heavy a shower of stones on the unfortunate intruders, that they either are killed on the spot or are compelled to retire, leaving their Messiah in his enchanted hiding-place.

XV.

Others, knowing that the Caspian hills were within our reach, and considering the fable of the Sabbatine river perfectly ridiculous, had recourse to Paradise, saying that the Messiah is entertained there in the company of Moses and Elijah; and that when the time should come, God would send him to deliver the Jews. To these two opinions may be added a third of the modern Rabbins, asserting that the Messiah has not come, nor ever will come, since God has not promised it in the Scriptures, nor is his advent an article of faith with the Jews. This newly invented opinion is so little followed, that as yet I have not met with any other person professing it, beside one Francisco Antonio de Olivares, a Castilian by birth, who was expelled this city the 14th July, 1686, and died professing this article of belief, or rather this absurdity, for such all the Jews uniformly consider it, as we read in the Talmud, Treatise *Sanhedrin*, chap. *Helek*, where the Rabbins expressly avow that there was no prophet who did not make mention of the advent of the Messiah: "*Omnes prophetæ aliquid de Messiah prædixerunt.*" The like is affirmed in *Yalcut* in the exposition of chapter lxvi. of Isaiah, p. 368. To this truth every Jew in fact bears witness, when on the Sabbath day, in all the Synagogues, they chant the celebrated Hebrew hymn *Yigdal Elohim Hay*, wherein they entreat God to hasten the advent of the Messiah. But not to dwell on an article that is acknowledged universally by every Synagogue, the testimony of Rabbi Moses of Egypt, one of the most ancient of the Jewish

Rabbins, will suffice to establish the fact. This Rabbi observes, in his exposition of the creed, that the eleventh article is the acknowledgment of the Messiah, in which the Jews are to believe with a perfect faith, under the penalty, in case they should reject it, of being reputed heretics by their Synagogues. "*Undecimus articulus est Messias, et hunc tenentur Hebræi firma fide credere et venturum sperare, prout omnes prophetæ predixerunt. Et qui hanc veritatem negaverit a lege discedere et hæreticum reputari deberet.*"

XVI.

These two opinions being premised, as those that the Jews hold concerning the Messiah, tell me, O children of Israel, was the Messiah who came at the period of the destruction of your city, or is the Messiah, who is, as you imagine, yet to come, to be a man or God and man united? This question being pressed, you will all reply that he was or is to be simply man. Then if such were your Messiah who has already come, or if such is to be the Messiah whom you still expect to come, know of a certainty none such will come, nor has yet come; for the Messiah whom you say is to be, or already has been, is totally impossible: and what is impossible cannot have happened in the past, nor can happen at any future time. The Messiah must be God and man; for God revealed to us by his prophets that the

Messiah was to possess the combination of the two natures, human and divine. And it is impossible that God should speak untruth, or that God should deceive; and it is equally impossible that there should be any true Messiah with other attributes than such as God revealed would appertain to the true Messiah. Therefore the Messiah whom your hopes induce you to imagine will still come, because he has not yet appeared, or the Messiah whom, notwithstanding his having already come, you still expect to accomplish your deliverance, is impossible in his very nature. Being impossible, he cannot have come already, nor can he remain to come; consequently, your expectation defeats itself, and will never be realized.

Hope, then, as long as you please, you who resolve to remain Jews; but undeceive yourselves, for if your Messiah was or is to be as you expect, he never will be nor has he been; for such a Messiah is an impossibility. Now hearken to your prophets.

XVII.

To the two prophets, Isaiah and Jeremiah, among several others, God revealed who was to be the Messiah that He had determined to send into the world. Isaiah, in the ninth chapter of his prophecies, described him thus, conformably to your Hebrew text: "*Infans natus est nobis, et filius datus est nobis, et erit principatus super hu-*

merum ejus: et vocabitur nomen ejus Admirabilis, Consiliarius, Deus, Fortis, Pater Sempiternus, [or *Pater Sempiternitatis*], *Princeps Pax; ad multiplicandum principatum et pacis non erit finis, super solium David et super regnum ejus sedebit, ut confirmet illud et corroboret in judicio et justitia a modo et usque in sempiternum.*" "Unto us a child is born, and unto us a son is given, and the government shall be upon his shoulders: he shall be called Wonderful, Counsellor, God, Powerful, everlasting Father [or the Father of Eternity], Prince of Peace [or Prince Peace]; whose empire shall be greatly augmented, he shall sit on the throne of David and over his kingdom, to establish and strengthen it in judgment and justice henceforth and to all eternity."

XVIII.

God made the same, or nearly the same revelation, with a slight difference, to the prophet Jeremiah, chapters xxiii and xxxiii, according to your Hebrew text: "*Ecce dies venient, dicit Dominus; et suscitabo David germen justum, et regnabit Rex et intelliget; et faciet judicium et justitiam in terra. In diebus illis salvabitur Juda, et Israel habitabit ad fiduciam; et hoc est nomen quod vocabunt eum: Jehova (seu Tetragrammaton) justus noster.*" "The time will come, says God, that I will produce for David a scion of his stock, he shall reign as king, shall be wise and shall execute judgment and justice on the earth; and in that time Judah shall be saved, and Israel shall unite with him in perfect confidence. The name he is to bear is that of God *Jehovah* (or the Tetragrammaton) our righteous one."

XIX.

These two prophets thus furnish, in their respective predictions, two signs, whereby you, as Jews, might recognise the promised Messiah.—Isaiah says, he is to be born a child: "*Infans natus est.*" That he was to be given at a certain time: "*Filius datus est.*" That he was to bear upon his shoulders: "*Super humerum ejus.*" That he was to hold the sovereignty which should increase and extend: "*Ad multiplicandum imperium.*" That he was to sit on the throne and be placed over the kingdom of David: "*Super solium David, et super regnum ejus.*" This is the first sign that the prophet gives, whereby to recognise the Messiah. But he says, moreover, that besides all these predictions, there will be another sign which appertains to the true Messiah, whereby he may be known. "For his surname shall be called, Wonderful (*Admirabilis*), Counsellor (*Conciliarius*), God (*Deus*), Powerful (*Fortis*), Everlasting Father (*Pater Sempiternus*), [or, Father of Eternity (*Pater Sempiternitatis*)], Prince of Peace (*Princeps Pacis*), [or, Prince Peace (*Princeps Pax*)]:"—that the peace should have no end: "*Et pacis non erit finis:*" that his empire should endure from now unto all eternity—"*A modo et usque in sempiternum.*" This is the second sign of the Messiah. The first sign clearly proves that the Messiah is to be man; for if the Messiah is to be born a child, to be produced in time, to bear on his shoulders an empire that will increase and extend, and be placed on the throne of David and over his kingdom, the Messiah must of necessity be man, for man alone can satisfy these conditions.

XX.

The second sign is a conclusive demonstration of the divinity of the Messiah, for if the Messiah is to bear the names that the prophet said he should, and to be called Wonderful, Counsellor, God, Powerful, Everlasting Father, or Father of Eternity, to hold perpetual sovereignty, kingdom without end and peace interminable: then, since no man who is only mere man, can have interminable peace, a kingdom without end, perpetual empire, nor be Eternal Father, or Father of Eternity, be called God, or have the name of God appropriated to him, it follows that the Messiah must be God, since these attributes can only belong to Him who is God. It follows, according to the first-mentioned conditions, that the Messiah must be man; and, according to the second, that he must be God; consequently, the Messiah must be both God and man.

D *

XXI.

The words of Jeremiah corroborate this argument, and also furnish two signs whereby the Messiah may be recognised; for he says, the Messiah was to be hereafter: "*Ecce dies venient.*" That he should appear in course of time: "*Suscitabo.*" That he was to be of the line of David: "*Germen David.*" That he should execute justice: "*Facit Justitiam;*" and that this justice was to be done on earth: "*In terra.*" That he should become king: "*Et regnabit Rex.*" That he should in time save the Jews: "*Salvabitur Juda;*"—and that the Jews are to live under him in perfect confidence: "*Israel habitabit ad fiducium.*" All these circumstances prove that the Messiah must be man, because with man only are these circumstances compatible.

XXII.

The Messiah, besides what we have already quoted from the prophet, was to be called by the proper name of God; and this name God was not to be any one indifferently of those applied to the Deity; but solely, that most sacred name *Jehovah*, which signifies in every way the existence of God and the essence of His eternity (as I shall presently prove from the Rabbins,) which name and the applied attribute are compatible with God alone. For inasmuch as it appertains to God alone to be self-existent, so to God alone can appertain this name which asserts His uncreatedness and His eternity: so that if God says, that this is the name the Messiah was to bear, either the Messiah must be God, or God places us in peril of adoring the Messiah as God, all the while that he is not God; since we should see the Messiah bearing as his proper name, that name which he could not bear unless he were God. God cannot be the cause of error or deception. According to the first-mentioned titles which God revealed the Messiah was to bear, he must be MAN; according to the second GOD: therefore the Messiah is both God and Man. Now, if you expect in the Messiah, man only, and not God, you expect an impossible Messiah. For the Messiah, upon that supposition, could not have those names ascribed to him which God said the Messiah should have. The prophets have told you that the Messiah is to be both God and Man; and you, in opposition to your prophets, through whose mouth God spake, expect a Messiah that is to be mere man. Thus you are expecting a Messiah that cannot have come, nor can ever have to come. So that your hope is self-destructive; for whereas no hope can be placed except upon a possible object, not only is the object which you hope for impossible, but equally so in its very nature is the hope itself, and is impossible to be realized either in the past, present, or future; so that your hope of a Messiah, merely man, is at the present time a dream, in the past a shadow, and in the future will prove a fable.

XXIII.

What solution do you give to these two prophecies that are so clearly adverse to your expectation? What answer do you make to a demonstration so decisive against your delusion? You must either believe or disbelieve what your two prophets have declared. If you believe them, how can you possibly expect a Messiah in contradiction to what they have foretold? If you do not believe them, why deceive the world, or why deceive yourselves by still calling yourselves Jews? I am well aware that you will answer me, that although as unlearned men you do not know how to reply to these prophecies, yet your teachers are perfectly competent to solve these difficulties, and that if you were in Holland, Venice, Leghorn, or Turin, we should not be able to press you so hard; for that in those places you have Rabbins, who, as men of education and learning, well know how to explain these passages, and are competent to reply to such arguments. Now I will stand in their place, and have only to request that you will consent to abide by the answers of your teachers and the exposition of your Rabbins, for I will repeat to you all that they write and teach with the object of throwing doubt upon our faith, in order that I may clearly demonstrate to you the falsity of their doctrines;

and I take God, who will judge us all, as witness, that I will relate to you all that your masters lay down, with a view to expound these difficulties; or rather, to use the words of your own Rabbi Samuel, I will repeat all your teachers have advanced, in order to deceive you and themselves. "*Domine*," says this rabbi, writing to Rabbi Isaac, "*Domine, mi videtur quod decipimus alios et nos ipsos.*"

XXIV.

Rabbi Eben Ezra, after he saw that he would be obliged, according to the text of Isaiah, to confess the Messiah to be God, fearing lest he should be cast out of the Synagogue, in order to keep in with the Jews, denied that the prophet spoke of the Messiah in that passage, alleging that the text alluded to king Hezekiah; and Rabbi Solomon, who was esteemed a *Solomon* among all the Jews, in order to deceive you, professed the same opinion; but perceiving that this interpretation would be easily refuted by the text, with a view to support his error, ventured to vitiate the original Hebrew, thereby committing a heavy crime, since there is an express command in Deut. iv. 2, wherein God forbids the committal of so wicked an act, "*Non addetis super verbo, quod ego præcipio vobis nec minuetis ex eo.*" So reads your Hebrew text. The modern rabbins explain in like manner, the passage in Jeremiah, for they also deny that the prophet spoke of the Messiah, some affirming that he alludes to David, and others to Zerubbabel; but all alike join in corrupting the sense of the text, and maintain that the name of God does not prove the divinity of the Messiah, for that it either is not ascribed, in the text to the Messiah, or even if it is so ascribed, the Scriptures show that the name of God is frequently applied to other objects besides the Deity.

XXV.

Such are the answers that your teachers make to our demonstrations; but these need only to be stated for their falsehood to become apparent.

Two false assertions are contained in the answers of your rabbins. The first, that those passages in Isaiah and Jeremiah were not intended to refer to the Messiah. The second, that, in the passage from Isaiah, the prophet speaks of King Hezekiah; and in that from Jeremiah, the prophet speaks of David or Zerubbabel. Moreover, that the name of God applied to the Messiah in these two passages, does not prove that the Messiah was God, even if they be allowed to refer to the Messiah; for that either the Messiah does not take upon himself the name of God, or even if he did assume that name, it would be no proof of his divinity. And that you may clearly see that the whole of this taught you by your rabbins is a gross falsehood and absurdity, I will show you with what ease their doctrines admit of refutation, and we will begin with showing that the two passages do refer to the Messiah.

XXVI.

The Targum, or Chaldee paraphrase of Rabbi Jonathan Ben Uziel, that is, Rabbi Jonathan son of Uziel, which some authors, evincing the little knowledge they had of the Hebrew writings, confound with the Targum of Onkelos, thus translates into Chaldee this passage of Isaiah following the text of the Hebrew. "*Infans natus est nobis, Filius datus est nobis, et suscipiet legem super se, ad conservandam eam, et vocabitur nomen ejus, Minkodam, Deus fortis, permanens in sæcula sæculorum Messiah.*"

This book is held so sacred among the Jews, that, down to the present day, no one of your Synagogues has ventured to reject or controvert it, not alone from its venerable antiquity (for it was composed one thousand seven hundred and forty-seven years ago, forty-two years before Christ), but because in all your schools which you improperly call "Synagogues," it is read every Sabbath day equally with the Torah, that is, the Pentateuch of Moses. Moreover, you or your rabbins (who have invented your ridiculous fictions,) have made your belief in this book a matter of public notoriety, from having had put into your head the well-known fable to the effect that when Jonathan was composing it, if a fly chanced to light on the paper on which he was writing, there came instantly a fire from heaven which consumed the fly, but left the paper untouched: a fine story for men of sense to believe in!

Now, if the Targum which is admitted as a book of infallible authority and as canonical, and the truth of which has been always held to be incontrovertible, explains the passage from the prophet Isaiah as relating to the Messiah, it must unquestionably be wrong in any Jew to deny that the prophet did not here allude to the Messiah.

XXVII.

The same sense as is given in the Targum, we find in *Beresheet Rabba*, in the large glossary on Gen. iv. where it says, viz :—" *Non est autem nomen Domini hic, nisi Rex Messias, ut dictum est: Principatus super humerum ejus!*" To these books which you hold as sacred and infallible, we will add the authority of the rabbins, to prove that the passage relates to the Messiah. Rabbi Joseph Galileo, in his preface to the Lamentations, which are called in Hebrew, *Echa Rabbathi*, being asked the name of the Messiah, answered thus—"*Nomen Messiæ Pax scriptum est, enim princeps pacis Moyses Egyptio.*" This rabbi, whom by distinction you call "the great preacher," also says in his epistle named *Igaret Teman*, written to the rabbins in Africa, " *Omnia nomina hic posita ab Isaia,* ix. *cum epithetis suis dicuntur de puero nato qui est Rex*

Messias." Consequently the opinions of Rabbi Eben Ezra, and of the other rabbins who deny that the passage treats of the Messiah, must be erroneous; for besides being in opposition to so many ancient rabbins it is contrary to the Targum, which you admit to be an authentic work, and even recognise as sacred.

XXVIII.

By the same evidence, it may be proved that the passage in Jeremiah is meant of the Messiah, which we consider to be the case not only because your most learned and most ancient rabbins who flourished in your synagogues acknowledge it, but because we find the same in the Targum of Jonathan. "*In tempore illo statuam Messiam justum et hoc est nomen quod ipsi dicent ei: Tetragrammaton justus noster.*" The same we infer from the book *Midrash Tehilim*, which is a commentary on the Psalms, where the text is thus expounded: "*Domine in virtute tua lætabitur Rex.*" Also in this book we read, "*Quod est Messiæ nomen est illud quod dicitur,*" in cap. xxiii. Jeremiæ, "*Dominus justus noster.*" The like we infer from the book *Echa Rabbathi*, where expounding that part of Lamentations, "*Longè factus est a me consolator,*" Rabbi Abba, speaking of the Messiah, writes thus: *Quia elongatus est a me consolator convertens animam meam. Quod est nomen Messiæ? Deus Jehova est nomen ejus, sicut dictum est*

Jeremiæ," cap. xxiii. "*Et hoc est nomen quod vocabunt eum, Dominus justus noster.*" This is proved from an infinite number of rabbins and books admitted by the Jews, which, in order not to waste time, I shall refrain from quoting. We are thus provided with a ready answer to your teachers, which proves them to be guilty of fallacy and falsehood in denying that these passages in the two prophets treat of the Messiah, because, they know not how to reply to the evidence of the demonstration we have given, and being determined to remain Jews, reject the interpretation both of the canonical books, and their most ancient rabbins, in order to persevere in error.

XXIX.

Eben Ezra and Rabbi Solomon, being thus convicted of falsehood, in denying that these prophets speak of the Messiah, we will now proceed to convict them of a second error in affirming that the passage in Isaiah applies to King Hezekiah, and also to expose the error of other Rabbins, in affirming that the text in Jeremiah alludes to David or Zerubbabel; and that the name of God applied in these two places to the Messiah, does not prove his divinity, even granting that they are applied to him: in other words, that the name of God is not applied to the Messiah, or even if so applied, is not sufficient to prove his divinity.

XXX.

First:—If the prophecy of Isaiah is to be understood to treat of Hezekiah, as these Rabbins pretend, they are bound to show us how the prediction of the prophet has been fulfilled in Hezekiah. But this they cannot show, as to do so they must either deny chapter xviii. of the 4th [2nd] Book of Kings, or must pronounce that the Scripture declares what is untrue, or has been falsified in this chapter. For if the prophet thus speaks of Hezekiah, of necessity Hezekiah was not called Hezekiah, but God; and this alone must have been his name. Farthermore, it must be shown that Hezekiah was the prince of peace, and the peace in his time was perpetual; also that he was Eternal Father, or Father of Eternity, and his dominion exists at this day, and will have no end; for all this can be inferred from the aforementioned passage in Isaiah, that he was to be the Son—born of Him of whom the prophet treats in chapter ix. Nothing of all this has been realized in Hezekiah, nor can be realized, but the direct contrary is shown in the sacred text. Therefore it is false to assert that the prophet speaks of Hezekiah.

XXXI.

That no one ever called Hezekiah a God, and that the designation of God was never bestowed on that prince, is most certain, because we cannot trace from Scripture that such title has been given to him; but, on the contrary, he is there never called by any other name than Hezekiah. That he never was nor could be the Eternal Father, or Father of Eternity, our natural reason is sufficient to convince us, for Hezekiah was notoriously a man; and it is incumbent upon your teachers to show when and how those epithets, which are the attributes of the Deity, were or could be rationally ascribed to Hezekiah; for none can be an everlasting Father, or Father of Eternity, unless his own existence were to all eternity, which is not the case with any other than the Deity. They must show us that this king and his generation exist at the present day, and that his dominion was multiplied, instead of being divided as it was, when he received it from his father. They must show us how the kingdom of David is strengthened and established at this day, and was not diminished and ruined in the time of his son Menasseh. But in order that this point may rest on more than mere assertion, we will establish it from the Scriptures.

XXXII.

The sacred text of chapter xviii. of the 4th Book of Kings, is quite opposed to this exposition of your Rabbins. Hezekiah was so far from extending his dominion, that he received only a portion of his father's kingdom. No sooner did he assume the reins of government than all the principal fortified cities of his kingdom were taken by Sannacherib; and in order to rid himself of the danger that threatened it, he gave the invader three hundred talents of silver and thirty of gold; and, to pay this tribute, was compelled not only to exhaust his treasury, but to withdraw from the temple the silver and gold which it contained. The peace conceded to him was of so short a duration, that his whole reign was a perpetual warfare; and finally his son lost the whole of his empire, and the establishment of the house of David came to an end in his person, in which the succession to the throne was lost and extinguished; since no other descendants of Hezekiah now exists, nor is the kingdom of that prince in being at the present day. All this happened to Hezekiah, as we see in chapters xviii., xix., and xx. of the 4th Book of Kings; and whatever is drawn from those chapters is an article of faith with you. Nothing of all this was to happen according to the predictions of Isaiah; therefore either the prophecy itself, or the account given in Kings, or the interpretation of the Rabbins, must be false. For if the prophet says that the One prophesied of was to be called God, to be prince of peace, and that to his peace there should be no end; to be Eternal Father or a Father of Eternity; that he was to have increased dominion; and that his kingdom was to be endless, and that he should perpetually establish the throne of David: then, since the passage in the Book of Kings informs us that every thing that happened to Hezekiah was contrary to what Isaiah had promised, it follows (if the exposition of this Rabbin is correct) that either the prophet, in what he has asserted, has spoken untruly, or else that the text in the Book of Kings is false in its statement of events. The prophet cannot deceive, nor can the text in Kings be disputed; therefore the fault must be with your Rabbins, who seek to verify in Hezekiah what is totally inconsistent with his character. And would you found your hopes on so palpable a fallacy?

XXXIII.

Unable to evade this dilemma, Rabbi Solomon and others have dared to vitiate the text of Isaiah and Jeremiah, in order to refute the opinion, that the Messiah was to be God, notwithstanding what the prophets declare to the contrary. Your Rabbins, seeing that, however they might labor to explain away the two texts, they could not keep out of view the divinity of the Messiah, in order to maintain themselves and you in the Jewish faith, laid down that the texts were not to be read as if the Messiah was to be called Powerful, Counsellor, Prince of Peace, or as if the name of God was the name the Messiah was to be known by, but as follows: *"Deus, Fortis, qui est Admirabilis, Concilarius, et Pater futu-*

ri Sæculi, vocabit Regem Messiah, Principem pacis," as if the Messiah was to bear the name of the Prince of Peace: and that God was not to be the Messiah, but to bestow on the Messiah the title of Prince of Peace; and likewise that the passage in Jeremiah should not be read thus—*"Hoc est nomen quod vocabunt eum: Dominus justus noster,"* but as follows: *"vocabit eum Deus justus noster,"* construing therefrom, that it is God who gave the name, and that the Messiah is the person named. These barbarians, by thus corrupting the former text, and substituting *vocabit* for *vocabitur* in Isaiah, and for *vocabunt* in Jeremiah, have concluded that the Messiah did not ascribe to himself the name of God; but they deceive themselves, for all this labor serves no other end than to prove their own falsehood and audacity. Of this I shall now proceed to give you the most ample evidence.

XXXIV.

In that passage of Isaiah where the word *vehicarè*, meaning *vocabitur*, occurs in the Hebrew, Rabbi Solomon, who was a notorious corrupter of the sacred text, has audaciously substituted *vahycrà*, which means *vocavit*. And in Jeremiah, where in the original *icreù* is written, which means *vocabunt*, he has substituted *icreo*, which means *vocavit*. It is a very easy matter to introduce such a corruption in the Hebrew; for, it should be borne in mind that the sacred text is always read without points; and even at this day the scroll of the Bible that is used in all your Synagogues is written without points; stops and punctuation only began to be in use in the Bible four hundred and seventy-six years after the birth of Christ, the first inventors being Rabbi Jacob Ben Naphtali, and Rabbi Aaron Ben Asser; the sacred books, before their time, having always been read without the points. When Christ came, the Jews, wishing to disprove his divinity, began to vitiate the Scriptures by means of the points. *Vehicarè*, that is, *vocabitur*, and *vahycrà*, which signifies *vocavit*, are written with the same letters (the points alone serving to distinguish them), and in like manner *icreo*, which means *vocavit*, is composed of the same letters as *icreù*, which means *vocabunt*. In order to corrupt the text in Jeremiah, they took the letter *vau*, which corresponds with our vowel *u*, and removing the dot which is placed in the middle of that letter, and makes *icreù*, they transferred it to another letter, so that the vowel *u* changes into *o*, and thereby converts *icreù* into *icreo;* thus, by the slight change of removing a single point from one letter to another, the text in Jeremiah has been materially altered.

XXXV.

In Isaiah the text has been altered as follows: *vehicarè* which is *vocabitur* or *vocabunt*, and *vahycrà* which means *vocavit*, are both written with the same letters. The vowel point *kamets* which was under the *coph* is transposed, and what was *vahycarè* becomes *vahycrà*. All this trouble and labor on the part of your rabbins, and among them Rabbi Solomon (whose chief business in the world seems to have consisted in leading you into error), you have thought fit to sanction. But we shall have no difficulty in confuting and exposing his falsehood; for if we refer to the Septuagint, which was written one thousand nine hundred and eighty-nine years ago, and about two hundred and eighty-four before Christ, and to the Targum, written one thousand seven hundred and forty-two years ago, or forty-two years before the birth of Christ, we shall find that they both read *vocabitur* or *vahycarè* and not *vahycrà* in Isaiah; and *icreù* (which is *vocabunt*) and not *icreo*, (*vocavit*) in the text of Jeremiah. Since, then, Jonathan who wrote in Chaldee, and the Seventy who wrote in Greek, agree in putting *vocabitur* in the first place and *vocabunt* in the second, it is beyond doubt that they must have been thus in the original which they translated. If you will not allow that it is so at the present day, it must follow that the text has been altered. That being supposed—

XXXVI.

Tell me dispassionately whom are we to follow, and whom to believe? Rabbi Solomon, who so many years after the birth of Christ tells us that in these passages we find *vocabit, vahycrà,* and *icrco,* in order to support his theory—or the Seventy interpreters, who were selected by the Jews exclusively from among themselves as the wisest men the Synagogue could produce, to render the Hebrew text into Greek, and who, notwithstanding they were separated from each other, agree in attesting, two hundred and eighty-four years before the birth of Christ, that the original text was *vahicarè* and *icreù,* as is proved by their rendering the words as *vocabitur* and *vocabunt?*

I again ask—in which of these two parties should we confide? In Rabbi Solomon, notorious for the immense number of the corruptions of sacred text that pervade his works, and who is comparatively but of yesterday?—or the Targum, written forty-two years before the coming of Christ, which uses in the Chaldee *vocabitur* and *vocabunt,* as corresponding with *icreù* and *vahycarè* in the original? Years and years before this rabbi wrote, the text was always read one way; and he was the first to propose that it should be read differently; can you then believe that he has delivered to you the truth? So many years previously to Rabbi Solomon's coming into the world, the texts were rendered in a different way from that in which he wishes they should now be read; consequently you must acknowledge it to be the fact that he has been guilty of corrupting them. With this demonstration before you, believe as you please. But if you prefer Rabbi Solomon to the Targum, and to the Seventy, you will act in opposition to that reverence in which both were ever held by the Synagogue.

XXXVII.

That the application of the name of God to the Messiah, in both these places, proves his divinity, is an argument which you and your teachers reject, urging that the divinity of the Messiah is not proved by the name of God having been applied to him, inasmuch as this name is applied in Scripture to many created objects; this is a ridiculous notion proceeding either from your ignorance or apostasy. We do not deny that the names of God are applied in Scripture to an infinite number of creatures rational and irrational, without proving thereby that such creatures are gods. But the point in question is, whether we cannot prove that the name *Jehovah*, which is more especially the name of God, and denotes that He is an Eternal Essence, is never attributed to any other besides Himself. If after that has been shown, we can demonstrate that this name has been assigned to the Messiah, it necessarily follows that he must be God.

XXXVIII.

If you are willing to discover the truth, let us carefully consult our Scriptures and yours. In the sacred book, ten several names are appropriated to God. "El," which signifies *Fortem*—"Sabaoth," which means *Lord of Valor* or *of Hosts*—"Serecie,"* which means *Misit me ad vos*—"Elyon" which means *Excelsum*—"Elohim," "Eloe," "Ja," "Adonai," which all mean the same as "Ja," which signifies *God*—"Shaddai," which means *Omnipotent;* and besides these, there is a more special name, Tetragrammaton, as it is called by the Greeks, or the ineffable Name of God, which the Jews call the name of four letters, *yod, he, vav, he.* Of these four letters or names is composed the most sacred name *Jehovah*, which is held so sacred among your people that, when you invoke the name of the Deity, you do not presume to utter the name *Jehovah* (except it be the High-priest on occasion of certain sacrifices), and on your hearing it pronounced, you prostrate your faces to the ground. Hence it comes, that when you meet this name in writing, you neither read nor pronounce it, but in its stead you substitute the word "Adonai." Neither you, nor the Greeks, nor the Latins, have as yet discovered its true signification. The Latins explain it by *Deus* or *Dominus*, the Greeks by *Tetragrammaton*, and the Hebrews by *Adonai*. And what is still

---

* "Serecie" is not Hebrew, and probably was intended for *Ehyeh* meaning *I am,*—see Ex. iii. 14, "I AM hath sent me unto you." [Or more correctly "I will be," as *Ehyeh* is the future, first person singular of *hayah*, to be.]

more, you wait for the Messiah to come, to know how it should be pronounced; for you say that he alone is acquainted with its true pronunciation. This being conceded, see what follows: The name Jehovah belongs exclusively to God, and signifies in the most explicit manner Self-existence, and as such cannot be communicated to any other than God (for with such a being alone is the attribute of absolute self-existence compatible). So that the Messiah must be God; for this name has been applied to him. All the other before-mentioned names, wherewith God is invoked, are ascribed to creatures, as you will find at every step in the Scriptures. But as regards the name Jehovah which has been applied to the Messiah, you cannot point out a single place in the Scriptures where it is ascribed to any other being except to the Messiah, and to God; to put this point beyond doubt, hear what Rabbi Moses says in his book called *Moré*, chap. vi.

"*Cuncta nomina Dei excelsi, quæ inveniuntur in Scripturis, ab aliqua certa operatione derivantur. Ad nomen istud, quod quatuor literis constat, nomen est particulare, et unicum Deo excelso, significatque Essentiam Divinam cum manifestá determinatione, ad solum Deum absque aliqua æqui vocatione et communicatione ad alterum qui Deus non sit.*" And in the same chapter he adds, "*Certê alia nomina Dei sunt nomina quæ declarant aliquam operationem à qua derivantur. At verò hoc nomen quatuor litera-*

rum non est cognitum ab aliqua derivatione et alteri non communicatur nisi soli Deo." Therefore if this name beyond all others, according to the Scriptures and the rabbins, is so especially the attribute of God, and is incommunicable to any other being, this name having been given to the Messiah, fully establishes his divinity; and your teachers, who well know the truth of what I am stating, purposely confound together the different names of God, with the express object of misleading you on this very point.

XXXIX.

To conclude this discourse, it only remains to prove the falsehood of the interpretation of your rabbins, in attributing to David or Zerubbabel the passage in Jeremiah. Observe, my brethren, that Jeremiah prophesied three hundred and eighty-six years after *David's death.* That prince, being dead, could not return to life, nor could he exist at a future time, having already existed in time past; so that if David was the subject of the prophecy, the prophet would not say that David *was to live* (*suscitabo*) but that he *had lived.* He would not say that he *should be* called (*vocabunt*) but that he *had been* called. He would not say that he *should sit* on the throne (*sedebit*) but that he *had already been seated.* Nor would he say he *should be* wise (*sapiens erit*) but that he *was* wise. He would not say that he *should be* king (*regnabit rex*) but that he *had been* king. He would not say that he *should execute* judgment (*faciet justitiam in terra*) but that he had executed judgment on earth, so that the prophecy would imply according to that interpretation, that David, who had lived, was again to appear. Consequently, the prophecy cannot be understood to relate to David. Much less can it be taken with reference to Zerubbabel, as may be shown, not by exactly the same arguments with which we have refuted the hypothesis of its applying to David, but by others equally convincing. Firstly, because the name *Jehovah* was not, and could not be applicable to Zerubbabel, as we have shown you from your rabbins. Secondly, the person prophesied of, was to be king (*regnabit rex*). Zerubbabel was not a king, whether you consider him under the Babylonian captivity or after he was restored to Judea. In the time of this prince, the people did not live securely under his government, which was another circumstance that was to appertain to the party prophesied of, "*et Israel habitabit ad fiduciam,*" for we learn the direct contrary from the Scriptures. The book of Esdras informs us, that, after the people were restored and were living under the government of Zerubbabel, they were in such a state of insecurity, that as they lifted up the stones to build the temple with one hand, they held the sword to defend their works in the other. Moreover after a short interval, Zerubbabel abandoned the government of Judea, and went back to Babylon; consequently the prophecy has not been verified in Zerubbabel. Thus easily may we refute the assertions of your rabbins; but the worst is, that, in spite of all the evidence we can produce, you remain unwilling to confess your error, and obstinately retain your belief in these false doctrines.

XL.

Be persuaded, my brethren, be persuaded to believe what your prophets have told you, and cease to cling to the absurdities which two ignorant rabbins have put into your head, and to which you only yield your belief, that you may have an excuse for remaining Jews. Resolve to open your eyes, and consent to be convinced by the truth; for you have too long allowed yourselves to be imposed upon by a falsehood. Acknowledge that you cannot obtain freedom so long as you do not change the nature of your hopes; for the redeemer you look for is impossible, because it is impossible to have a Messiah without his being both God and man. This has been foretold you by the prophets, as you have already heard; and the like is affirmed by your rabbins, as you shall now hear; for in this opinion the most learned men, your Synagogue ever had, are of one accord.

XLI.

Rabbi Hosea, in the opinion of some, or Rabbi Simeon ben Jochay, in the opinion of others, who flourished many years before the birth of Christ, being two of the most ancient rabbins of the Synagogue—in expounding the prophet Hosea, speaks thus: "Woe to the impious and homicidal Jews, who shall murder the Messiah, the Son of God; for there be those who when God sends into the world his Son, the Messiah, to pardon their sins, shall resist and put him to death when he comes." "*Deus sanctus et benedictus mittet Filium sanctum suum et carne humana se induet; væ illis impiis homicidis Israel, ob quorum amorem mittet Deus Filium suum, ut eis peccata dimittat quia propter pravas suas opiniones erunt rebelles huic Messiæ et ingenti iracundiæ perciti eum occident.*" This is what your rabbi tells you you would do to the Messiah who was the Son of God. And what more do we say? If the Messiah was the Son of God, and this Son of God clothed himself with human flesh, according to what this Rabbi has acknowledged so long before the Messiah appeared, must not the Messiah have been both God and man? In so far as he was God, you could not slay him; but in so far as he was man, you did slay him. Thus the Messiah was both God and man.

XLII.

Rabbi Haccadosh, whom by distinction you call the Holy Rabbi, and who flourished one hundred and twenty-eight years before the birth of Christ (for he lived in the time of the Maccabees), in his celebrated work, called in the Hebrew *Gala Razeya*, which signifies the revealing of secrets, speaking of the Messiah, in his exposition of the 9th chapter of the prophet Isaiah, which we have just explained, writes thus:—"*Quia Messias Deus et Homo futurus est, ideo vocatus est Emmanuel, quod interpretatus nobiscum Deus.*"— "Because the Messiah has to be both God and man, therefore he shall be called Emmanuel, which means God with us." He repeats this truth still more clearly in another passage, as you will find on referring to a Hebrew work which you call *The Gates of Light*:—"*Rex Messias componitur ex Divinitate et Humanitate, et in substantiâ Regis Messiæ inveniuntur duæ filiationes quarum una est Divinitatis, quâ Dei filius est, altera erit humanitatis, quâ erit filius prophetissæ. In Messia substantia Divinitatis distincta erit a substantia humanitatis et e contra. Quæ duo simul juncta sunt in Messia.*" "The King Messiah," says this rabbi, "is composed both of humanity and divinity; for Messiah has two filiations, one partaking of divinity, by virtue whereof he is the Son of God: the other filiation as of the nature of humanity, and by virtue of this he will be the son of the prophetess. The Messiah consists of two substances, each different from the other. One is divine, the other human. But these two substances, in themselves distinct, become united in the Messiah.

The prophets and rabbins who lived before the advent of Christ explicitly declared that the Messiah was to be both God and man; and it was only in consequence of your stubborn resolution to remain Jews, that you denied Christ to be the Messiah, and resolved to look out for another of a character different from what your prophets and rabbins had previously laid down. From all this, it becomes evident that the coming of the Messiah is an impossibility. The Scriptures cannot err, nor can your rabbins, men enlightened by God (who before the advent of Christ declared these truths), be guilty of falsehood. Therefore Messiah cannot come as simply man; consequently, the Messiah whom you so anxiously expect is impossible, because the essential attributes are wanting in him which God revealed the Messiah should possess. For these reasons your redemption cannot take place, seeing that the Messiah is impossible, who, according to your expectations, is to redeem you. Thus your tears are fruitless, for your hopes do not rest upon one who can put an end to your captivity. Thus it is that you find yourselves, and must remain till the end of the world, in the condition in which we now see you (which is exactly such as your Isaiah prophesied) without there being any one to redeem or ransom you.—"*Ipse autem populus direptus, et vastatus, laqueus juvenum omnes, et in domibus carcerum absconditi sunt; facti sunt in rapinam, nec qui est eruat; in direptionem, nec est qui dicat: Redde.*"

XLIII.

Impossible as it is, that he whom you expect can be the Messiah, for want of the essential attributes which were to belong to him, the event is rendered equally so by the period in which the true Messiah was to appear; for that period is expired and can never recur. The time for the coming of the Messiah was accomplished and fulfilled when Christ came; and any farther fulfilment is obviously impossible Unhappy people, whose hopes, not only the nature of the object, but the time appointed for its fulfilment, alike conspire to defeat.

XLIV.

To convince you of this truth, satisfactory proof may be adduced from the prophecy of Jacob, in Genesis, chap. xlix., when, desirous to point out to his sons the time of the advent of the Messiah, he tells them that the time of his coming would be when the sceptre should fail in your nation. Now in fact it did fail when Christ came, for Herod the Ascalonite held the sceptre. Supposing that you should now or hereafter, be told by some sinful or ignorant Jew, that this text is not a convincing argument, for that long before the advent of Christ, the sceptre had failed in Jeconiah: this can only be said by one totally ignorant of sacred history; for after Jeconiah,

Josias reigned; and although after this prince, the title of king was lost to the nation until the time of Herod, still the government of the Jews was preserved with equal authority in the persons of their princes, as is most clearly set forth in the Scriptures. To prove still farther this article, the prophecy of Daniel in chap. ix. gives evident demonstration that his weeks, however you may attempt to dispute the computation, are already accomplished. There is scarcely a sermon on the same subject, in which these two texts are not brought under discussion; but in order that you may not allege that we Catholics are so deficient in proofs for your conviction that we are obliged to make the same arguments serve many times, I will not allow myself to dwell on the above texts, but shall be enabled by others of equal evidence, to show you the futility of your hopes, and to convince you that the time has past which you are expecting, under the belief that the Messiah has not yet come, but is still to appear.

XLV.

The prophet Daniel, chap. ii., relates Nebuchadnezzar's dream, wherein he saw a statue, of which the head was of gold, the arms of silver, its belly of brass, its feet of iron and clay. He also saw a small stone thrown from a hill, which, striking the feet of the statue, reduced it to powder. The head of the statue represented the empire of the Chaldeans; the arms, that of the Medes and Persians; the belly, that of the Greeks; and the feet, that of the Romans. Such is the interpretation given by your prophets and rabbins. The last named empire, namely, the Roman, (continues Daniel, chap. ii. 3,) will be mixed, one part being iron, and the other part clay. On this account, although the clay may mingle with the iron, the two parts can never unite; for, however closely mixed up, they will not adhere to each other, inasmuch as the clay will not amalgamate with the iron, nor the iron with the clay, "*Commiscebuntur sed non adhærebunt sibi.*" And this was verified; for the Roman empire, which was typified by the iron, and the clay, which was the kingdom of the Jews (says your Rabbi Joaô Baptista Deste, who, after recognising the error of your belief, turned Catholic), although mixed, did not unite; for the same power was not possessed by the clay, which was your kingdom, as by the iron, which was that of the Romans. A like exposition has been given by your Rabbi Fabiano de Tioghi (who also became converted to Christ after being expelled from the Synagogue), in his book named *Dialogo de la Fede.* Thus, the prophet says that these two powers should be intermingled (*Commiscebuntur*), but should not be united (*sed non adhærebunt sibi*). Allowing that the Jews and the Romans confederated together as friends, they ever preserved a separate government; for, until the reign of Herod the Ascalonite, in whose time Christ came, the temporal government of Judea was held by the Jews. The Romans became your allies in your defence, and you united with the Romans to afford them assistance; but in religion you were totally at variance; for among you was established the worship of the true God, but among the Romans a blind idolatry. These facts are certain, and admit of no doubt or dispute; for we and all the world know that they are recorded in the Book of Maccabees, where we are informed of the confederacy you made with the Romans, while you still continued to maintain the observances of your law, and the government of your kingdom, until the friendship between you becoming relaxed, the Romans sent Herod to govern you, in company with others in their confidence; and subsequently wishing to make an end of you, sent to destroy your city.

XLVI.

At the time that the iron of the Roman empire was mingled with the clay of the kingdom of the Jews, a small stone, says the prophet, destroyed the iron and the clay; and in their place a kingdom arose, that should never be destroyed or surrendered to any other power, for its dominion was to be throughout the world, and its rule over all the earth, and to endure to eternity (Dan. ii. 11). *" In diebus regnorum illorum suscitabit Deus cœli regnum quod in æternum non dissipabitur, et alteri populo non tradetur. Cominuet autem et consumet universa regna hæc, et ipsum stabit in æternum.*" This is the prophecy from which we collect, that the empires of the Chaldeans, Persians, and Greeks being destroyed, but the Roman empire still existing (that is to say, the iron) mingled with the kingdom of the Jews (that is the clay), another kingdom or empire was to arise that should destroy both these powers; and that the empire which should succeed the two so destroyed, was to hold perpetual dominion, unaffected by time, and should never pass into other hands, since the stone that destroyed the several empires, in order to establish the one that was to arise from their ruins, would increase to such an extent that its bulk would fill the whole earth. "*Consumet universa regna hæc, et ipsum stabit in æternum; secundum quod vidisti, quod de monte abscissus est lapis sine manibus, et comminuet testam et ferrum, et œs et argentum et aureum.*"

XLVII.

That this prophecy of Daniel treats of the Messiah, is a settled point among your rabbins: so it is acknowledged in the book *Midrash Tehilim*, which is a commentary on the Psalms, in the exposition of Psalm xvii. 44, 45. "*Quando Messias veniet, non erunt dicentes canticum, donec cadat coram ipso habens, digitos, id est, regnum Romanorum de quo dictum est Daniel secundo; et digitus ex parte ferrei, et ex parte teste, ex parte regnum solidum et ex parte frivolum. In diebus regnorum illorum statuet Deus cœli regnum quod in æternum. Iste est rex Messias sicut dictum est in* Bereshith Rabbà."

The same we read in *Bereshith Rabbà,* in the commentary on Gen. xlii. *"Rex verò nonus est ipse Cæsar Augustus, qui universo orbe imperavit, sicut dictum est Daniel secundo, et regnum quartum erit forte sicut ferrum. Rex decimus est Messias qui regnabit a fine mundi, usque ad finem ejus, sicut dictum est, lapis qui percussit statuam, replenit universam terram."*

The same thing is affirmed by Rabbi Naham, Rabbi Moyses Hadarsan and Rabbi Soadias in the same place, *"Lapis qui percussit statuam est regnum Messiah filii David."* Now it being admitted, that this interpretation is written in your books, and acknowledged by your rabbins, we will proceed to give you a clear explanation of this your prophecy.

XLVIII.

The Messiah, according to what the prophet says, was to come when the Roman empire should be still mixed up with the Jews; and the advent of the Messiah was to destroy equally the clay of the Jews, and the iron of the Romans; for out of the ruins of these two kingdoms the kingdom of the Messiah was to arise, which was to be everlasting and to spread throughout the world. Now either this prophecy must be false, which you will not assert (for Daniel was a true prophet), or the period for the Messiah's coming must be already passed, seeing that the Roman empire is not at this day mixed with the kingdom of the Jews, nor their kingdom with that empire; for both these powers have been destroyed. If this is denied, you will be driven to maintain, either that these two powers still exist united, or that the Messiah did not come during the period when the mixture of the Romans and the Jews continued.

If you admit that the Messiah was not to come during that time, your prophet speaks falsely, which surely you will not admit; and your rabbins must have also deceived you, which you will be equally unwilling to acknowledge. If you allege that these two powers are still flourishing and under a joint government, it will be obligatory on you to show us whereabouts this kingdom exists, and in what part of Judea or of the world at this day, you still hold dominion. You will have to give the lie to all the world and to yourselves; for you and every body else are well aware that your kingdom was destroyed sixteen hundred and thirty-two years ago, and that your dominion is at an end in Judea; nor is there any part of the earth where you now hold rule. It is evident, therefore, that you have now none of these things remaining which were to exist until the birth of the Messiah. Then how can you expect the Messiah to come after it has been proved that he has already appeared? The Roman empire mixed with yours is passed away, and not a vestige of your kingdom remains. The kingdom that was to succeed these two powers has been established for a long period of years, and has diffused itself throughout Europe, Asia, Africa, and America. It follows then that the time which the prophet assigned for the coming of the Messiah is past: and being past cannot be expected back again. Thus your expectations are in direct variance with the period assigned for that event.

XLIX.

There exists only one difficulty in this explanation; but this difficulty arises from the scanty knowledge you have of the Scriptures. By this prophecy we learn, that the Messiah, when he should come, was to found his own kingdom by destroying the kingdom of the Jews and the Roman empire. But the latter still subsists, and is not destroyed; consequently it would seem as if the period for the advent of the Messiah had not yet arrived. This argument proceeded from the infamous Henriques, called Miguel Henriques among us while he pretended to be a Catholic, and Michael Henriques among you, after he declared himself a Jew, and as such suffered punishment in this city on the eleventh of May, 1682. That such an opinion has become current amongst you is the fault of your voluntary blindness, for you voluntarily adopt a false interpretation of the sacred text. The Messiah was not to destroy the Roman empire in a physical sense; for, had the prophet spoken of such a kind of destruction, it is very evident he would have committed a great absurdity in affirming that a small stone, and which fell without hands from a mountain, was to annihilate a power whose dominion extended throughout the world, and that the same stone should afterwards itself grow into a mountain to fill the whole earth. The prophet then spoke of a spiritual destruction, and the annihilation of the religion and idolatry which the Romans practised. With the advent of Christ, idolatry ceased in all the countries into which the Romans had carried their religious worship; and thus the religion of the Romans was extinguished throughout the world, so that, on Christ's coming, their empire was spiritually destroyed. I will now proceed with additional arguments in evidence of this truth.

L.

The Messiah was to destroy the Roman empire, as we learn from the prophecy, in order to found his own. But the empire of the Messiah was to be spiritual; therefore the destruction which was to precede it must be so too. I will prove the major of this syllogism, which alone requires proof. The kingdom of the Messiah according to the prophet, was to be everlasting, "*Stabit in æternum.*" It was never to end, for it was never to be destroyed, "*In æternum non dissipabitur.*" It was not to descend to others, "*Alteri non tradetur.*" No temporal or material object can be prevented from descending to others, or fail to come to an end.

The kingdom of the Messiah, which was to be eternal and perpetual (for it was never to devolve upon others), could not mean a temporal kingdom. Consequently it must have been a spiritual destruction of the Roman empire which was to be effected by the Messiah, since the kingdom of the Messiah that was to follow this destruction was spiritual. The fact is, that the spiritual dominion of the Roman empire absolutely ceased on the advent of Christ; for the idolatry of the Roman empire terminated throughout the world on his coming.

Thus Sophonias prophesied. Sophon. chapter xx. v. 17. "*Horribilis Dominus et attenuabit omnes deos terræ.*" This is also admitted in your Talmud, in the book Zohar. Rabbi Moses of Egypt contends for the same thing, affirming that Jesus of Nazereth was a good man, because he put an end to idolatry throughout the world: "*Jesus Nazarenus fuit vir bonus, et destruxit idolorum adorationem.*" Therefore, if, according to your rabbins, your Talmud, and your prophet Sophonias, this was the kind of destruction that the Messiah was to effect when he came, and which the true Messiah, Jesus Christ, actually did effect: it follows that the destruction of the Roman empire, predicted by Daniel, was of a similar character, and must have therefore been intended in a spiritual sense.

LI.

In order more thoroughly to convince you, I will treat all the evidence in the very way that you have adopted as most favorable to your own erroneous views, and will be even more liberal than your commentators who have treated upon this passage. I am willing to grant that the Messiah was to bring a temporal destruction on the Roman empire, and will show you as clearly as the light at noon-day that this temporal destruction has already come to pass; for, after so many victories gained by the Turks, and the repeated triumphs of its enemies, how can it be asserted of this empire that it still flourishes? The Roman empire, as long as it endured, held dominion throughout the world, subjected kingdoms, exacted obedience from princes, and exercised universal jurisdiction. Nothing of this any longer exists, as you must yourselves allow. This is sufficient to show that the Roman empire is already, even in a material sense, destroyed. This government, to which in former days the whole world was tributary, now possesses so small a revenue, that deducting what arises from conquest or inheritance, which is the appanage of the reigning imperial house (not of the empire), that which remains is not sufficient for the maintenance of the emperor, I will not say with the dignity due to his rank, but even as a private nobleman; for if they were at this day to elect an emperor who happened not to possess property of his own, he would be unable to maintain himself with all the revenue the empire could furnish. This is an evident truth, and shows that the temporal dominion of the Roman empire is effectually destroyed. How then can you hope that the Messiah is still to come when this fact proves that he has already been? It can only be from your reluctance to relinquish your visionary hopes, that you employ these futile arguments, and because you have no better reply at your command, but are still at all hazard determined to remain Jews; it would cost you less trouble to renounce the authority of your prophets, than to have recourse to these miserable evasions. However, if you are indifferent to the voice of your prophets, you will perhaps attend to what your rabbins affirm; for I wish to show you by the doctrines of your own teachers, that the advent of the Messiah is an event not still to be expected, but one already past.

LII.

Consult your Talmud, Treatises *Sabat* and *Sanhedrin*, and there you will find that Rabbi Tanhuma asks the reason why the Hebrew word *Lemarbé* is used by the prophet Isaiah, chapter ix., to express "*multiplicandum ejus imperium,*" and why the final ם (Mem) is placed in the middle of the *Lemarbé*, when it is contrary to usage to put such letter in the middle of any other Hebrew word. No one has yet been found who could solve this question; and accordingly it is said in your Talmud, that he heard a voice from heaven answering him thus, *Razi-li, Razi-li*, which Hebrew words translated into Latin mean "*Secretum meum mihi;*" "*Secretum meum mihi;*" or, My secret is my own; My secret is my own. It is assented to by many of your teachers that from the time of Isaiah's prophecy in chapter ix., until the advent of the Messiah, a period of six hundred years was to elapse. Now let us see how many years have really elapsed since that prophecy down to the present time, and when these six hundred years were, or will be, fully completed, in order that we may discover whether your Messiah has already come, or is still to come, as calculated by your rabbins. The better to convince you, I will follow no other chronology than that adopted by them.

LIII.

The date of this prophecy was in the fourth year of King Ahaz, reckoning from which time down to the eleventh year of King Zedekiah, according to the computation of your Rabbi Salomon, one hundred and fifty years had elapsed. In that year, the first temple was burnt, and you were carried captive into Babylon. From the destruction of the first temple to the destruction of the second, by the account of that same rabbi, four hundred and ninety years had passed, which number added to one hundred and fifty, makes six hundred and forty one years. From this we must deduct the forty-one years since the death of Christ. Consequently, agreeably to the computation of this rabbi, the year in which Christ died completed the six hundred years elapsed since the prophecy of Isaiah; and this was the period in which the Messiah was to come. It is now one thousand six hundred and thirty-two years since the time when Titus destroyed your city. Between that period and the fourth year of Ahaz six hundred years intervene, so that from the prophecy until the present day we may reckon two thousand two hundred and thirty-two years; deduct the six hundred, and the advent of the Messiah, conformably to your Talmud, should have taken place one thousand six hundred and thirty-two years ago. And thus, although one thousand six hundred and thirty-two years, by your own computation, must have taken place since his advent, you still go on expecting him to come. Moreover, you do this in open contradiction to your Talmud, which no one can venture to oppose without incurring the penalty of death;

such being the punishment awarded by that book, to those who deny any part of its contents.

LIV.

I invite you to consult the Talmud, book *Sanhedrin Guazit*, chapter *Col Israel*, and you will there see the period which your rabbins cabalistically assign for the advent of the Messiah. The Jews have two and twenty letters, by which they reckon their numbers. When they are placed in a manner that does not make sense, like our A B C, they stand for numerals. The first letter א (Aleph), corresponding to our A, means the number *One*. The second ב (Beth), means *Two*. The third ג (Ghimel), *Three;* and so forth to י (Yod), which means *Ten*. The next letter כ (Caph), means *Twenty;* and so on increasing by tens to ק (Koph), which is *One Hundred;* ר (Resch) means *Two Hundred;* ש (Shin) *Three Hundred;* and ת (Tauv), the last letter, stands for *Four Hundred*. The Hebrews make use of all these letters, not only in common writing, but in expressing numbers in arithmetic and in all computations relating to the Messiah. They begin with taking the first and last letters, Aleph and Tauv; and the intermediate ones between Aleph and Mem joined to these three make in all six hundred and five, so that the final or closed ם, as we have already stated, contains within itself the secret of the Messiah's advent, indicating as it does the six hundred years corresponding to that event. These have already elapsed; and consequently the Messiah has already appeared.

LV.

Rabbi Moses' Ben Maimon, in his celebrated epistle to the rabbins of Africa, states, that by an ancient tradition of the Hebrews, the Messiah was to appear in the year of the world four thousand four hundred and seventy-four. We are now, according to your computation, in the year five thousand four hundred and sixty-five, from the creation of the world, so that if the Messiah was to appear in four thousand four hundred and seventy four, it must be nine hundred and ninety-one years since he came, and consequently you are expecting him all this time after he has already been.

LVI.

In the Talmud, chapter *Helek*, in the *Sanhedrin Guazit*, as well as in *Sedar Holam*, we find it written, that the world is to endure only six thousand years: "*Machina mundi hujus annorum series mille et non plurum persistere debet.*" So also affirm your rabbins, according to ancient tradition, originating with the disciples of Elijah. The first two thousand years with the law of nature and without a written law; the second two thousand years with the law of Moses; and the last two thousand years with the law of the Messiah. The two thousand years under natural law have long since passed away; the two thousand years under the written law are also passed; consequently the two thousand under the law of the Messiah alone are wanting. According to the computation adopted by your people in calculating the age of the world (which puts us in the year five thousand four hundred and sixty-five from the creation of the world), we are now in the final two thousand that belong to the Messiah, out of which five hundred and thirty-five have already expired. Consequently, your own reckoning shows that you are expecting One who came five hundred and thirty-five years ago.

LVII.

Rabbi Elijah son of Rabbi Judas, a Talmudist of the highest authority with you, writes thus: *"Non minus octoginta quinque jubilæa mundus stabit, et in ultimo veniet Messias."* The world then is to exist during eighty-five jubilees; and in the last the Messiah is to appear. Your Rabbi Salomon, in explaining these eighty-five jubilees of the world's duration, says, according to Scripture, that each jubilee consists of fifty years, and the whole together amount to four thousand two hundred and fifty: *"Octaginta jubilæa faciunt annos quatuor mille ducentos et quinquaginta annos."* By this computation the world is to exist four thousand two hundred and fifty years, and in the last jubilee, that is, in the last fifty years, the Messiah was to come. It is evident, therefore, that the

Messiah came one thousand two hundred and fifteen years ago; for that is the number of years that has elapsed from the year four thousand two hundred and fifty to the present time. Then how can you expect a Messiah, who, by your own reckoning, must have appeared so long since? He was to come during the last jubilee, when the world should have existed four thousand two hundred years, and be about entering the last fifty, which were to complete the period of four thousand two hundred and fifty years. Being then at present in the year five thousand four hundred and sixty-five, can you suppose the time for the Messiah's coming not yet arrived? If you reflect on the force of this argument, you will doubtless take the advice of your Rabbi Samuel, who, convinced by this reasoning, renounced your creed and acknowledged Jesus Christ. "*Stupeo, ac credo Jesum verum Dei Filium extetisse Messiam, et jam venisse; revolvendo Scripta prophetarum, manifestè intelligo Christum esse Dei Filium nobis in terram missum ad redemptionem nostram.*—I am amazed at this," said the Rabbi, "and believe that Jesus, the true Son of God, was the Messiah, and has already come. For, revolving in my mind all that the prophets have said, I clearly understand that Christ is the Son of God, who was sent into the world to redeem us." This Rabbi acknowledged the truth by renouncing his former belief, and you would do well to follow his example. Rabbi Anima Voluntas, or Rabbi Moses of Egypt, who is the same person, also acknowledged this truth, as we may infer from *Sanhedrin Guazit*, in *Helek;* for the Jews inquiring of him the time of the Messiah's coming, he (reflecting on the procrastination of his own and your expectations of this event) answered them as follows: "*Vanum est atque inanè a Judaicis Messiam expectari, sed sola redemptio consistit in pœnitentiâ.*—It is perfectly in vain," says this Rabbi, "for the Jews to expect the Messiah; for at this time it is only by repentance that they can obtain redemption."

Undeceive yourselves, therefore, my brethren, as your rabbins have already done. Undeceive yourselves, and admit that your hopes are fallacious, and that the advent of the Messiah is already passed, and having passed cannot come again; but if you are not satisfied by this consideration which was sufficient to satisfy your rabbins, I would ask you in conclusion what reply you can make to the following question?

LVIII.

Do you know how many Messiahs have appeared in the world whom you have received without raising any difficulty or dispute? If not, as probably is the case, I will enumerate all that have come to my knowledge. Before the birth of Christ, Theudas declared himself to be the true Messiah. The Jews received him publicly; and four hundred Jews assembled in Jerusalem, who, being persuaded that he could conduct them over the River Jordan dryshod, followed him with all that belonged to them. This being made known to the Roman garrison who commanded the city, they went out and destroyed him and his followers, and re-entered Jerusalem carrying the head of Theudas in triumph. So relates your historian Josephus. This was the first Messiah whom you received without any difficulty or controversy, and having acknowledged him as such, you paid with your lives the forfeit of your credulity.

LIX.

About the time of the birth of Christ, there came another Messiah, Judas Galileo, who prevailed on you not to pay tribute to Cæsar, when he had ordered a general impost to be collected throughout the world. The whole Jewish people received him with transport, but you and Judas your Messiah experienced the same fate as Theudas. After that again, in the time of Felix the Proconsul of Judea, came a third Messiah, named Egipcio, who was received by you with equal delight, and having instilled into your minds the idea of ridding Jerusalem of the yoke of the Romans, with four thousand men sought to obtain possession of the city, but being opposed by Felix, he and his followers met the same end as the two former Messiahs. Some short time after this, came two new pretenders, named John and Simon, who found equally ready acceptance with you as the rest, and led you to the same disastrous consequences. After the death of Christ, a sixth Messiah appeared, named Barcosbas, or as some called him, Bencosbas, or as others will have it Barchossiba, who gained over the most enlightened man the Jews possessed at that period (namely, Rabbi Akiba, as we learn from the Talmud), and succeeded in inducing you to rebel against the Romans; which resulted in your destruction by Titus and Vespasian. Forty-eight years after this event, a seventh pretender appeared, named Ventozora, whom some erroneously supposed to be the same as Barchossiba. Under his persuasion, having fortified yourselves against the Romans in Bithera or Bither, your country was again ravaged by Adrian, who brought destruction upon you and your pretended Messiah.

LX.

In the course of time came an eighth Messiah, named Mahir, who was received by you with your usual alacrity, and caused you to pay dearly for your acceptance of him. The ninth Messiah appeared in Sicily, and made you believe that he was to lead you like Moses through the sea; and having obtained credit with you, he and all who followed him found their grave in the waters. In the year sixteen hundred and sixty-six came the tenth Messiah, named Sabbati Essevi, who with the greater part of his followers was condemned to death by the Turks at Constantinople. And that this country might not prove an exception to your notorious credulity, there came a Jew from India, known in our history by the name of the Jew of Zapato, who told you that he was the Messiah, and that having announced himself publicly to the Jews on the Euphrates as such, he had come to you to declare the good tidings, whereupon you eagerly ran to receive him, expecting through his means to gain possession of the Indies; the matter, however, ended in his being quickly laid hold of and imprisoned by the Holy Inquisition.

Josephus mentions three Messiahs more, Judas Gaulonitis, Judas son of Ezechias, and Athronges, a shepherd, all of whom met the same fate as those who went before them.

LXI.

Here we have fourteen Messiahs publicly received by you as such. Now tell me, I entreat, when you acknowledged each of these as the Messiah, had the time arrived for his coming or had it not? If not, how could you receive these as such before the time appointed? If the time had arrived, and on that ground you received them, how can you affirm that the time of the Messiah's coming is still distant? How can you maintain that the time was come when all others might be Messiahs; but that for Christ alone the time was not yet come when he might be the Messiah?

What answer can you make to this demonstration? what else but simply to acknowledge that you are convinced, for such a demonstration precludes any other reply: either you must confess your error, and admit that, on the score of time, the advent of your Messiah is impossible, or totally shut your eyes to reason, from an obstinate determination to remain Jews. Cease to act thus, my brethren; for if such be your resolution, no greater misfortune can befall you: your captivity will still endure, your exile be prolonged, and your oppression become more stringent every day; for a Messiah can never come to relieve you, seeing that the time for that is already gone by, consequently there can be no end to the misfortunes with which your prophets have menaced you: "*Ipse autem populus direptus et vastatus; laqueus juvenum omnes, et in domibus carcerum absconditi sunt; facti sunt in rapinam, nec est qui eruat; in direptionem, nec est qui dicat, Redde.*"

LXII.

We are now arrived (slowly, it is true, but our progress would have been still slower, had I advanced all the proofs which I had prepared for this sermon),—we are now, I say, arrived at the third part of our demonstration, in which I have to prove to you that the Messiah, the object of your fervent aspirations, and whom your obstinacy has continued to expect for so many years, is impossible by reason of those signs that were to belong to him, all of which have been already accomplished in Christ, and having been so accomplished, do not admit of being fulfilled a second time. There was to be only one Messiah: that is acknowledged by all your ancient Rabbins; and I have not time to dwell on this point, which it is of the less consequence to do, as it is not called in question by any of your modern teachers. The Messiah was to be one person; but, if at different periods the same signs have been fulfilled in two persons that God gave for one only, the Messiah must necessarily be two, for there could be no better reason that the Messiah should be one rather than the other. This cannot be the case; for God promised the world only one Messiah: besides, if at different times we perceive altogether the same signs in two Messiahs, as belong to one only, God has deceived us in having accomplished in two those signs which were proper only to one. It is impossible, as our natural reason suggests, that God should deceive us: consequently, it is impossible that at different times the very same signs should be realized in two persons, because one of these two would have been the true Messiah and the other false. But since the signs would have been found in both, which could properly belong to one alone, the other would be, and would not be the Messiah. He would be the Messiah, because manifesting the signs prophesied; and he would not be, because two Messiahs were impossible. Moreover, if there were two Messiahs at different times accompanied by the same signs, a man could not but be held guiltless who should worship either of the two, although that one should chance to be the false Messiah, the very same signs being apparent in both, and there being no reason in favor of the one above the other.

The Messiah, whom God commanded us to worship as his Son, is one; and to no other Messiah but him is similar worship due. This is expressly stated in the sacred text, according to the original Hebrew: *"Osculamini,"* or *"adorate Filium ejus, ne forte irascatur Filius ille, et omnino pereat qui illius viam non sequitur."* And where would be the justice of God promising only one Messiah with certain infallible signs, should He confer these very signs on two different persons? This argument proves most conclusively that the Messiah whom the Jews expect can never appear, and annihilates the grounds upon which their hopes are founded, seeing that the signs, that God revealed should accompany the Messiah, began to be realized one thousand seven hundred and five years ago in the person of Jesus of Nazareth, and it is now one thousand six hundred and thirty-two years since they were fully accomplished, such being the number of years since your city was taken and destroyed under Titus.

LXIII.

To complete this demonstration, I would inquire whether you expect your Messiah to come with the signs described by your Scriptures and prophets, or with others unknown to us and yourselves? You surely will not say that you expect any others besides those revealed from God; consequently, he must come with the signs we collect from Scripture. All these, without one single discrepancy, have been fulfilled in Christ; therefore in no one but Christ can they again be fulfilled. Now let us examine, not all the signs, for that is impossible in a single sermon, but only the principal ones which God revealed should be manifested in the Messiah.

LXIV.

One of the signs of the Messiah, God says by the prophet Isaiah, chapter viii., was, that when the Messiah should come into the world, the ruin of the Jews and the destruction of their city should follow: "*Et erit vobis in sanctificationem, in lapidem autem offensionis et in petram scandali duabus domibus Israel; in laqueum, et in ruinam habitantibus in Jerusalem.*" In the Chaldean paraphrase (or) the Targum of Jonathan, we read: "*Et erit vobis Messias in scandalum duabus domibus Israel.*" If you deny that this sign belonged to the Messiah, or that the prophet spoke with reference to him, you contradict the Targum and the Talmud; for the commentary upon this passage in the Treatises *Sanhedrin* and *Yalcut*, evidently assumes that the Messiah is the person alluded to: "*Non veniet filius David quousque non consumentur duæ domus patrum Israel, sicut scriptum est in Isaiah*, (chapter viii.)" The same is affirmed by your Rabbi Salomon in his exposition of Micah, chapter v., "*Iste dominator est Messias filius David, de quo scriptum est: Et erit in petram scandali.*" Two signs, says the prophet, shall witness to the Messiah. He is to be a stumbling-block to the Jews, and the Jews are to be ruined in their dominion and city on his advent. This being granted, I call upon you to declare whether these signs were or were not fulfilled in Christ? If they were not, why were you so greatly offended in Christ, that as the cause of your offence you persecuted and crucified him? Why do you continue at this day to be offended in him, so that you cannot without offence bear to hear him named? If he did not satisfy the predictions, how is it that your city is destroyed? If he did verify them, how is it that you hope for the Messiah, and seek for his coming, that you may crucify him? You have already done so, and would you go on, from day to day, murdering your Messiah? Why do you seek or hope for him? Is it that your kingdom may be lost?

It is already lost. Is it that he may be the destruction of your city? The Romans have already destroyed it. Is it that he may deprive you of the government of Judea? It is already taken from you. Is it that he may be an offence and stumbling-block to you? Already you have stumbled over and been offended in him, since you put him to death as a criminal, though he was innocence itself. Let us enlarge upon this point: and tell me if the Messiah, whom you expect, is to be an offence and stumbling-block to you; and will he bring ruin and destruction upon you?— You will all answer, No; for the Messiah is to be the object of your adoration, submission, and respect. Your Messiah is to restore you to freedom, reinstate you in your city, conduct you in safety to Judea, and give you once more the dominion of Palestine. Well, is such to be the Messiah you are looking for? If so, he will be a false Messiah; for the true Messiah was to put an end to your dominion, destroy Judea, ruin your city, and be an opprobrium to you, as your prophet and your rabbins agree in foretelling.— Now, your Messiah will not bring with him these tokens: and, consequently, Christ must be the true Messiah; and he whom you expect to come after Christ, must be a false Messiah.

LXV.

From Isaiah we pass to the text of Hosea, upon which we shall only bestow a cursory glance; for if we were to dwell upon it, it would be sufficient in itself for a whole sermon. The prophet Hosea in chap. iii. gives us other signs whereby the Messiah might be known on his coming. *"Dies multus expectabit, et ego expectabo vos."* When the Messiah comes, says the prophet, the Jews will be expecting him, and the Messiah will be expecting the Jews; and as the Jews were not to receive him, they should remain without a king, without a prince, without a sacrifice, and without an altar, *"Sedebunt filii Israel, sine rege, sine principe, sine sacrificio, et sine altari."* And after long remaining in this condition, they would acknowledge their error, and in the latter days worship the Messiah, whom they were not willing to accept when he came. *"Et post hæc revertentur filii Israel ad Dominum Deum suum et ad David regem suum."* You cannot avoid the force of the prophecy, by maintaining with some of your rabbins, that the passage does not allude to the Messiah, but to David; for your own Targum, a sacred book with you, interprets the passage as relating to the Messiah, *"Post hæc obedient Messiæ filio David."* And your rabbins acknowledge that the Messiah is understood in Scripture under the name of David, as we learn from *Medrash Mishle*, a Glossary on the Proverbs in chap. xix. and from the book called *Zohar*, in the exposition of chap. xix. of Leviticus. Moreover, independently of the doctrine of your rabbins, it clashes both with reason and with Scripture, to suppose that the passage can be explained as relating to David.

LXVI.

It clashes with Scripture, for it there appears that David died many years ago; and it clashes with reason, since it is evident that as David is dead he cannot expect you, nor can you expect him while the world exists. For it is clear that David after his death cannot return, and, consequently, you cannot expect him, nor he you, for the dead cannot expect the living. Thus it is proved the prophet did not speak of David. You have to expect him who was predicted, "*Expectabis me.*" He is also to expect you, "*Ego expectabo vos.*" If he is to expect you, then he must have already come; for if he had not come you might have continued to expect him, but he could not have to expect *you*. You cannot expect David, for he has already appeared; nor David expect *you*, seeing that he is dead: consequently this prophecy cannot be understood to allude to David. Moreover you are to seek out the person predicted as your God. "*Quærent Dominum Deum suum.*" None of you are now looking for David, for he has appeared long since, nor do you acknowledge David to be God. Thus your exposition must be untrue. Besides, you were to deny the person predicted; but subsequently at the end of the world, to be converted to him, "*Post hac revertentur.*" You were to adore him

I

as your God, says the Targum, "*Revertentur ad cultum Dei sui.*" Thus he whom you were to deny, when he first came, was God. David you did not deny, at the time when he came; nor will you worship him as your God, at the end of the world, when he may come to life again. Therefore David cannot be the person foretold by your prophet Hosea.

LXVII.

Much less can you refer the application of this prophecy to the Babylonian captivity; for in the captivity of which your prophet speaks, you were not to have a king, a prophet, or priest. In Babylon you had a priest named Josedek, as we perceive in Daniel xiii.;* you had kings and princes, priests and sacrifices. All this is corroborated in Baruch† i. 10; you had sacrifices and priests, "*Facite manna, et offerte pro peccato ad aram Domini Dei Nostri.*" You had a king, namely, Joachim; you had princes, namely, Zerubbabel and Salathiel; consequently, the prophet did not speak of the Babylonian captivity. This being granted and accepted as certain, as also that the prophet spoke of the Messiah, we will now proceed to the consideration of these signs in Christ Jesus.

---

* The Hebrew canon has no such chapter, Daniel ending with chapter xii.

† This book is also apocryphal.

LXVIII.

Is this prophecy true? You cannot but acknowledge its authenticity, and that, consequently, the Messiah has already come; for, otherwise, the Messiah could not be expecting you, *"expectabo vos."* He came, you would not receive him; and for this reason you have neither prince, altar, sacrifice, nor priest; you are to turn to him, *"Revertentur;"* you are to seek for him, *"Quærent Dominum Deum suum."* Have you to return to him? Then you must have turned away from him when he came. Has the prophecy been verified or not? If it has not been verified, how comes it that you did not receive Christ when he came; and that you are since without prince, altar, sacrifice, priest, or king? seeing that you were to be reduced to this state, in consequence of not accepting the Messiah when he should come. If these things have been already accomplished, how can they ever be accomplished again? Will you reject your Messiah when he shall appear? You will all reply in the negative, consequently in him, the signs of the true Messiah cannot be fulfilled, for the true Messiah when he came was to be rejected by the Jews. Thus if the signs are incapable of being hereafter verified, it is because they have already been verified in Christ. But it is impossible that they can be so again; and, consequently, the Messiah whom you expect becomes impossible. On the advent of *your* Messiah, are you to lose king, sacrifice, and prince? This cannot be; for all these things are left to him to restore to you. Thus, in your Messiah, this sign cannot be fulfilled; therefore Christ, in whom it was fulfilled, was the Messiah, and he whom you look for will never exist. To what end do you expect and hope for a Messiah? Is it to reject him? You have done this already. Is it that you may be left without king, prince, sacrifice, altar, or priest? You have been in this state sufficiently long already; and if on his coming you remain so, the Messiah you expect, as we have fully shown, cannot be the true Messiah.

From Hosea we turn to Malachi to discover another sign of the true Messiah, which has already been fulfilled, and therefore cannot occur again. Malachi i. 10, *"Non est mihi voluntas in vobis. Munus vestrum non suscipiam de manu vestra. Ab ortu enim solis usque ad occasum, magnum est nomen meum in Gentibus, et in omni loco sacrificabitur mihi oblatio munda."* When the Messiah comes, God said through the prophet Malachi, the person of the Jews shall no longer be agreeable to me, nor will I desire to receive their sacrifices; for, from the rising of the sun to the going down thereof, my name shall be great among the nations (that is among the Heathen), and in every place a pure sacrifice shall be offered to me. This being certain, from prophecy, tell me, are not yourselves and your sacrifices rejected? Have not the gentiles entered into possession of your heritage? Does God accept any sacrifice or external worship from you? Is there any part of the world where the converted heathen do not offer sacrifice to the true God? You can deny no part of this, for it is manifest to the whole world. The whole world knows it to be true, that you do not now offer sacrifice; that it is a tenet of your faith not to offer sacrifice out of Jerusalem. All the world knows that your sacrifices and yourselves are rejected, and that you have neither altar nor priest. All the world knows, as well as yourselves, how you bewail, with unavailing tears, that we gentiles are in possession of your heritage. All the world knows that there is no country on the globe, where the converted gentile does not adore the true God, and offer up sacrifice of the most pure worship and acceptable oblation. Either this prophecy has been accomplished or not. If not, sacrifice cannot exist throughout the world, but only in Jerusalem. This is not the fact; for although Jerusalem still exists, there is no one place in the temple where you are permitted to offer up sacrifice. If the prophecy is not fulfilled, the prophet must have spoken untruly, and you cannot avoid conceding, without falling into a palpable contradiction, that, according to your view, he is mistaken in two events, which he affirms were to occur at the same time. First, that

God would reject and put an end to your sacrifices. Secondly, that after this rejection, the gentiles throughout the world would offer sacrifice. You do not now offer sacrifices, as yourselves allow, and, as you obstinately maintain, neither do we; you must admit one of these two alternatives, either that the prophet has spoken falsely in declaring, that whenever the sacrifices of the Jews should cease, those of the gentiles should follow; or else, that yours having ceased, ours have already begun. The first alternative you cannot maintain; consequently, you must acknowledge the second. Besides, if we do not at the present day offer sacrifice, you place yourselves in a dilemma, as it would show that God now receives, nowhere throughout the world, either sacrifice or adoration; for *you* do not render any, still less the Mahomedans. And if you should maintain that *we* do not, it follows that there are none in the world who offer sacrifice in the true worship of God. This is impossible; consequently, the sign predicted has already occurred, and does not remain to be verified. To what purpose do you hope and seek for a Messiah? Is it to forfeit your right of primogeniture? That is already lost to you. That the gentiles should possess your inheritance? This they already do. That God should reject you? Already you have been rejected. Are all these things to happen when your Messiah comes?—

Are you to be rejected? Are you to lose your inheritance and your right of primogeniture?—You will answer me in the negative; for, that your Messiah is to restore you to all those things of which you have been deprived during your captivity. So that your Messiah, who is to come, will never appear, or if he were to come, cannot be the true one; for, on the advent of the true Messiah, all things were to be lost to you. Now open your eyes, my brethren, for I have not time to produce other proofs—open your eyes, and yourselves behold the miserable condition in which you now are, and perceive how fully all the signs have been verified in Christ Jesus that the prophets gave for your direction in ascertaining the true Messiah. You have brought your misery upon yourselves, by your refusal to accept the Messiah, and because, instead of worshipping his person, you took his life on the cross. This was your sin, and for that you are at this day suffering punishment, as acknowledged by Rabbi Samuel, *"Non paveo quod peccatum, per quod sumus in hac captivitate, sed illud propter quod locutus est dominus per Amos; expavesco, quod iste Jesus sit ille Justus venditus pro argento."*

LXX.

Adopt, then, the conclusion of this eminent Rabbi, and at length undeceive yourselves; for it is full time, seeing that your hopes are but an empty shadow, the Messiah you expect a chimera: and any Messiah but Jesus of Nazareth is a dream and an absurdity; for Christ alone possessed all the true qualifications that were predicted of the Messiah, and it is impossible that any other person can be invested with the same. Be satisfied that any Messiah but Christ is impossible; for Christ having come, the time is past for the advent of any other. Understand, finally, that any Messiah beyond the person of Christ is an impossibility, because all the tokens of the real Messiah have already been fufilled in him.

If you will repent with all your heart, and sincerely admit this conviction, happy indeed will you be in renouncing your error; for, with a knowledge of the truth, you will abandon the shadows of the Synagogue for the light of the church, the horrors of heresy for the beauty of faith. Take comfort; for, although chastisement may have placed you in the right road, it will, in the end, have been the instrument of opening your eyes; and you will find your God so merciful, that although, as Jews, you rejected him for your Father, on your repentance he will again receive you as his children, having redeemed you by his own precious blood. Prove yourselves, in the true sense of the word, good Jews; for if "Jew" means one who makes acknowledgment, you ought to acknowledge your errors, if you would be thought truly to remain Jews. The honor you have lost by coming under the sentence of the Inquisition, and the property that has been confiscated on account of your heresy, you will recover, accompanied with great grief of heart, on account of its not being by misfortune that you have incurred so much suffering, but for your sins and offences against a God to whom you are so much indebted.

LXXI.

And you, unhappy man, who stand here among these penitents, if you would obtain remission for your sins, open your eyes in time, that the fire in which your body is to be consumed may not extend, at the same time, to consume your soul. O beloved son of my heart, redeemed by the blood of Jesus Christ, educated in the bosom of the Church, bathed in the holy waters of baptism, O that I could, with the best blood of my veins, cure you of your blindness; for, were that possible, I would shed the last drop to remove your illusion, and rescue your soul from the power of the devil, who renders you thus obstinate. How bitterly do I grieve at your misery; and how deeply is my soul plunged in sorrow at beholding you in imminent peril of eternal condemnation! Consider, my son, begotten in the gospel, born among Catholics,* and illuminated by the

---

* The preacher evidently alludes to some noted person, whose name it is in vain to look for with the little information at our command.

light afforded you by so many learned men, consider how greatly you are deceived, and that if you have the misfortune to die in this condition, a consuming fire awaits your soul, to envelop it in flames to all eternity, after a temporal fire has already consumed your body. You are convicted of being a Jew from direct evidence; and you have yourself confessed your guilt, thinking to diminish the crime by confession. Besides this, you have lapsed into the abominable error of Atheism. Now reconcile, if you can, these two things, of being at the same time an Atheist and a Jew. If at this day salvation could be obtained by the Law of Moses, which it cannot, you are in the wretched condition of being out of the pale of salvation; for you will die a heretic to the very law you profess. You are a Sadducean Jew, as you have yourself acknowledged. Are you ignorant, that even at the time when your law still existed, the opinions of the Sadducees were considered heretical, inasmuch as they denied the doctrine of the resurrection, and consequently the immortality of the soul? You are still in a worse state, for you do not only deny the immortality of the soul, but are so blind as to deny having a soul. You affirm that there is no other happiness beyond this world—that life is the only true salvation—and that perdition is not in hell, for there is no such place, but death is the sole destruction. If you believe (however erroneously) this to be the fact, why do you seek to lose a life in which alone happiness consists in your opinion? How can it be your pleasure to die, if death, in your judgment, is the only perdition? Suffer yourself to be persuaded by one who ardently desires your salvation. Entreat the mercy of the tribunal of the Holy Office, which with so much compassion has waited two years, and has so patiently borne with your vacillation, at one time repenting, at another time retracting, and finally settling down into the miserable dogma of Atheism. Confess your errors, not with the desire of preserving your life, but with the simple view to the salvation of your soul. But if your are determined to die in your present state, I summon you hence to the day of judgment, when both of us, having risen from the dead, shall appear in the presence of the true God. You will return to life as a Jew and a heretic, in which state you die: I, on the other hand, hope for the divine mercy by returning to life as a Catholic, because, I trust through the divine goodness, I shall die in the law of Jesus Christ, in which alone salvation can be obtained. We both of us have to appear, at the resurrection, in the presence of the Supreme Judge; and you will then see that God may reprove me for the greatness of my sins, but will not for being false to my faith. He may reproach me for my defective observance thereof, but not for my want of sincerity therein; unless God were unjust, which he is not. But as to you, he will not only judge you on account of your crimes, but will condemn you for the observance of the law in which you died. Imagine yourself in the presence of God, free from any other sin than that of persevering in the law of Moses; and imagine a Christian in the same divine presence, free from any crime but the observance of the law of Christ. If God were to condemn the Christian for the love of his law, and grant salvation to the Jew for a similar observance on his part, God would not act with justice, nor would it be reconcilable with those reasons which we Catholics urge in proof of his justice. For in that case the Catholic might reason with God as follows: "Upright Judge, I believe in Christ, because he fulfilled all those signs that you revealed by your prophets, that your Son should be invested with. I acted as you commanded me; and you now condemn me for so doing. Why will you condemn me for being obedient?" Assuredly, this statement will not admit of any contradiction. Consequently, it is impossible that God will condemn the Catholic for remaining a Christian.

Now let us suppose a Jew, whom God condemns for his observance of the law of Moses, attempting to argue with God against his judgment. He would say: "O God, I believed in the

God of Abraham, Isaac, and Jacob; I observed the law you gave to Moses, then why condemn me?" But then God might reply: "You speak untruly; for Abraham, Isaac, and Jacob believed, and expected a future Messiah, who was to be my Son, and was to possess all those signs that I promised, whereby he might be known. This Son came into the world, and in him were apparent all the tokens revealed in the Scriptures.— You were so far from acknowledging or believing him, that you crucified him. The law given to Moses was to come to an end with the advent of my Son, and he was to promulgate another, which was to spread throughout the whole world; and you saw with your own eyes the signs of the time in which this law was to be promulgated. (John xv. 22.) If my Son had not come into the world, and the prophecies had not been accomplished, you might be excused, by saying you observed the law that I gave forever, and that you believed in the God of Abraham, Isaac, and Jacob. But now that every thing has been satisfactorily fulfilled, I am just in condemning you, and you are rebellious in remaining a Jew." My brother, however frightful this may be that I am now reciting to you, such will be indeed your lot on that day. Such is the mesh in which you, of your own choice, will be caught. This is the net that you are now weaving for all connected with you, your children, your parents, your relatives, your friends, and your entire race, for such is the wretched lot foretold by your prophets. "*Ipse autem populus direptus, et vastatus; laqueus juvenum omnes, et in domibus carcerum absconditi sunt; facti sunt in rapinam, nec est qui eruat; in direptionem, nec est qui dicat: Redde.*"

LXXII.

I have come to a conclusion with my proofs, and likewise with you, O unhappy people of Israel. O God, my Lord, who was crucified by the Jews, as much for their salvation as for our good, Lord, soften their obdurate hearts; for there stands a heart truly obdurate among these wretched people. Though they took up stones from the road to kill you, now that you have suffered death, subdue the hardened hearts of the Jews who murdered you, and still refuse to love you; you bestowed sight on a blind man, who put a spear to your side, give eyes to this blind people who still desire to pierce you, and still point the spear to your heart. Sprinkle, O God of my soul, sprinkle anew water and blood from your compassionate heart over these wretched men: it may be they will repent, seeing that a heart offended by such repeated provocations still lavishes favors so little deserved by their repeated transgressions. You rent the veil of the temple in token that your death put an end to the Jewish Synagogue: rend the veil that has covered the Jewish heart for so many years, that with all their heart they may renounce their errors through the saving influence of your death. You have awaited with open arms the sons of Judea for seventeen hundred and five years, and the more eagerly you solicit them to come to you, the more ungratefully they turn away from you, and obstinately refuse to acknowledge you as their Messiah. I know how anxiously you desire to save them, that you died forever in dying for them, and that they for murdering you are in danger of perishing eternally. Be mindful, O Lord God! through your compassionate nature, be mindful of these your sons, who, in fact, are of your own blood, and whom you redeemed at the price of so much suffering. They were so ignorant, that though you were their Father, they would not admit themselves to be your sons; but the ingratitude of children ever finds pardon in the love of a parent. You called to them in kindness, but they made an ungrateful return for your favors. Seek now to win them to you by chastisement, however little chastisement has hitherto benefited them. Cause them to acknowledge, with perfect sincerity, that in their present miserable state they have no other remedy than to repent for the time they have

lost in their false expectations, by bewailing their errors, abhorring their sins, abominating their superstition, and renouncing their contumacy; so that, being regenerated by the waters of their penitent eyes, they may be born again your children, as already by baptism they have become.

LAUS DEO!

This Reply was written by David Nieto, born at Venice, in 1654. He was a physician, judge & preacher at Leghorn and died in 1728 as the Chacham of the Portuguese congregation of London. The preceding "Respuesta al Sermon predicado por el arcobispo de Cangranor" was printed after his death at Villa-franca (London) in octavo, without date "por el autor de las noticias reconditas de la inquisicion" M.S.

REPLY TO THE SERMON OF THE ARCHBISHOP OF CRANGANOR,

AT

THE AUTO DA FE,

SOLEMNIZED IN LISBON, SEPTEMBER 6, 1705.

BY

THE AUTHOR OF THE SECRET HISTORY OF THE INQUISITION,

A POSTHUMOUS WORK PRINTED IN VILLA-FRANCA,

BY

CARLOS VERO.

J*

INTRODUCTION.

I OUGHT to inform the candid reader, that the reply to the sermon I am now about to publish, is the posthumous work of an eminent person known in the republic of letters by his excellent and judicious productions; and although his advanced age and tormenting infirmities little disposed him to engage in controversy, yet, to comply with the wishes of some of his friends who were most anxious to see a refutation of this boasted sermon, he composed that which is hereto subjoined, and quoted the several articles of the sermon separately, in order to reply minutely to each. His intention was not to attack the Christian religion, but to defend his own; and to show that the calumny which the archbishop has promulgated against that most eminent and learned writer, Rabbi R. Solomon, of having corrupted the text of the holy Scriptures, should actually be ascribed to the archbishop himself, or to some Christian who preceded him. That the author has accomplished his object, he who will read and examine the sermon and the refutation without being blinded by prejudice or interest, cannot fail to acknowledge; and I am persuaded that any one capable of weighing the reasoning of each party, will perceive an immense difference between the sermon and the reply; since all the reasoning the sermon presents is deduced from the erroneous conclusions and conceits of its author, from inaccurate quotations, allegory, and words wrested from their literal sense; while the reply is composed of real and true inferences, deduced from premises founded on clear and evident prophecies, explained in the literal sense, without being perverted from their natural meaning, or frittered away by typical interpretation, in order to make them suit a particular purpose, as practised by the preacher in his sermon.

So much it has been considered necessary to state to the friendly reader; for most people desire to know something of an author as well as of his work.

There is nothing more useful to religion than free discussion. We ought closely to search and examine into the subject, with a view to establish it on the most solid foundation; but whoever wishes to form a just opinion, must divest himself of all the prejudices imbibed by education, and reflect that his opponent has a soul as well as himself, and is desirous to attain that supreme felicity, which is the aim of all true religion; he ought to consider that there is no man in the world who, if he knew that there existed a true religion, which was not his own, but would abandon his own and embrace the true one; for if he did not, his obstinate opposition to his own good would render him unworthy of the title of Man.

This being admitted, it follows, that if the motive which stimulated him to controversy, is to bring over to what he believes to be the true religion those who, for want of being rightly informed, have been kept away from it, he ought to avail himself of those means which best conduce to the desired effect; he should adopt the most persuasive style, and confine himself to strict reasoning, solid arguments, to inferences correctly deduced, and to conclusions carefully drawn; he ought not to evince any partiality except for truth, but should acknowledge reason wherever he may meet it, and exhibit perfect sincerity and candor throughout; he ought to flee from subterfuge and fiction; be most scrupulous of what he ventures to assert, and honest in giving the correct sense of his quotations; he ought not to offend by using ignominious terms, nor invent calumnies to uphold his doctrine, much less claim a victory founded on passages perverted from their literal meaning. It is in this manner that the discussion will be best conducted, and the truth most easily elicited, which is the object we ought to seek. To act otherwise serves only to endanger the credit of the disputant and the religion he advocates; for when we find that a man is unable to defend his creed without offering offence to his opponent, and resorting to calumnies and falsehood, we are apt to attribute the defects of the pleader to the religion itself, and naturally conclude, that since no other argument but abuse has been put forward, none other can be advanced; and the opposite party, instead of becoming converted, only remains more firmly attached to his own faith.

Religion being a matter that so vitally concerns every human being, on entering into polemical discussions, with the view of converting another person to our creed, no language unworthy of learned and rational men should be resorted to; otherwise, instead of following up the investigation of the more essential principles in question, we should be occupied in resenting the insults offered, and in framing others in retaliation, by which means hatred and ill-will are engendered, instead of the amicable feelings that ought to prevail.

I am of opinion that we ought to esteem and respect any person who attempts to convert us to his own religion, whatever that may be, which (according to his belief) will procure for us the greatest and most exalted benefits that man can desire; and if he treats us with the courtesy consistent with the sincerity to which he lays claim, we ought to endeavor to answer him in the most courteous and charitable terms in our power; but, on the other hand, nothing forbids us to hold in contempt, and to regard as outcasts from the republic of letters, those who wilfully pervert facts and disfigure the truth to answer their own purposes.

All the religions in the world admit of being classified under four denominations. The first, comprehending the greater part of the world, is made up of the various Pagan religions which suppose a multitude of gods, or no god at all; the next, less numerous than the Pagans, although more so than those which follow, is Mahomedanism; the third is Christianity, embracing fewer disciples than those above named, but more than the fourth, which is the least of all in number. This consists of those who profess the Jewish religion.

As we have not much knowledge of the various Pagan creeds, it is unnecessary to take them into consideration; the rest (namely, Mahomedans, Christians, and Jews) agree in the opinion that there exists only One Sole Eternal Cause, that created, directs, and governs the world; moreover, Christians and Jews coincide in maintaining that none other but their respective religions can be true.

Now, the Jewish religion may be divided into two forms of faith: the one professed by the majority of the Jews is the Law of Moses conjoined with rabbinical traditions; the other is that which is professed by the Caraites, who reject tradition.

It would be necessary, therefore, for a Christian disposed to become a convert, and to be convinced of the truth of the Jewish religion, before professing either of the two creeds, to examine with every possible accuracy and diligence the reasoning of both parties, in order to know in favor of which he should decide; since if he remain uninformed of the arguments on which either is founded, he will not be in a position to discover the truth; but, after acquiring a minute and extensive knowledge of the ground of persuasion that prevails with them each to follow their respective opinions, he will then be master of the question, and competent to choose the side he deems best supported. I cannot conceive how any Jew can conscientiously be induced to become a convert to Christianity, without first examining most rigidly all the various opinions that have been and still are entertained among the professors of that creed, as well as the reasons which are urged for and against them; for on this subject there exists so great a diversity of judgments, that each party claims the victory for itself, and remains persuaded that it alone professes the true religion, and that all others are mere schismatics. What man is there so learned, so acute, and so thorough a theologian that he can presume to decide for one sect in particular, much less to fix his choice, without first well weighing and comparing together the various opinions?

This is a task which ought to be performed among Christians themselves; nor should any of them presume to decide on the subject, who had not first thoroughly examined into every sect of his religion, divested of the prejudice resulting from having been brought up in a different mode of belief. To convert the Jews, therefore, it would be requisite, in the first place, to call a general council of all the professors of Christianity, under whatever denomination they may be styled, not excepting the Unitarians; and when the general council shall have agreed which of all their various opinions ought to be adopted by common consent of all, uninfluenced by artifice, deceit, interest, or arbitrary power, it would then be proper to summon another council, to which the Jews might have free access and full liberty to deliver their opinions explicitly, without fear or reserve, on a subject involving the salvation of all.

The Christians should first prove that Christ was the promised Messiah from the Old Testament, and from all the prophecies which speak literally of the true Messiah, without perversion or allegory. They must produce authority for asserting that He was to be both God and Man.— They must prove from the Old Testament that God is *One* and Three; they must show clearly the obligation of the Jews to renounce the Law of Moses, and to embrace that of Christ, and satisfy us by what authority this latter law was ordained; and after all this, they should patiently attend to the arguments which we might allege to the contrary. Each party should have full liberty of speech and reply, and be ready to acknowledge the truth, on whichever side and under whatever form and circumstances it might appear.

This is the only way to bring all to acknowledge the truth; but to produce that effect, it would be requisite that such a council should be open to the public without restriction, that it should be composed of men not holding any religious appointment from either party, so that no one might be constrained to persist in his own particular creed for the sake of retaining office.

It appears to me that it is only in this manner the truth can be elicited, and a decision come to on the question that has been agitated during seventeen hundred years, and which may subsist, God alone knows how much longer.

But it is as great madness for the archbishop to believe that the Jews will yield their opinions under the influence of subtlety and allegory, as it would be for them to believe that he would yield his, so long as the church has any benefices to bestow. Let each man adhere to his own creed, and worship God with an upright and pure intention, and not depart from what has been taught him (provided he does not feel competent to decide for himself), and leave to God the care of his salvation. He, who is all-merciful, will accept his upright intentions, although his form of creed may not be the most acceptable. Let theologians talk as they please, this is what I shall ever believe; for I can never be persuaded that our merciful Creator will withhold His grace even from an upright and virtuous Mahomedan, who observes his religion, because he sincerely believes it to be the best manner in which he can worship God.

THE SERMON REFUTED.

PARAGRAPH II.—"*You are the persons whose patience has never been exhausted by long protracted hope.*"

Righteous Heaven! How great must be the force of that prejudice, which can presume to censure as a crime the practice of a virtue so truly heroic, and so well deserving the highest encomium.

It is on account of this sublime hope, that the people of Israel are called a holy people; for neither captivity, banishment, martyrdom, affliction, or degradation has been sufficient to make them abandon the true faith; nor has the hope of future greatness or present prosperity proved an adequate incentive to make them renounce their sacred and imperishable religion; such is their constancy in truth and such the strength of their belief, that, preferring heavenly to all human considerations, they do not, and will not forsake God and His law.

In a similar case, doubtless, the noble preacher and his followers (since he deems the patience and hope of the Jews so great an evil) would think it more becoming to sacrifice patience and hope, and turn away from one deity to another, and from one law to another, as they are wont to do with their saints, fixing their devotion upon those from whom they anticipate the most prompt return.

But to show the archbishop how much God esteems this virtue, and in what terms He extols it, let them attend to the words of the prophet Jeremiah ii. 2, where it is affirmed that he will not forget the patience with which the holy people followed him forty years in the wilderness: *"Recordor tibi benignitatis adolescentiæ tuæ, amoris sponsalium tuorum, te prosequitam esse me per desertum, per terram non satam."*

If the Divine Majesty was thus pleased with the dependence on His divine providence during the short term of forty years, how much more so must He be with their patience and endurance during so many centuries of captivity and exile?

"You are those to whose minds the clearest evidence does not bring conviction!"

In proceeding to proofs, the force of this evidence will be examined.

VI.—See the prophet Isaiah, chap. xlii.

The preacher imagines that the prophecy alluded to describes the calamities, extortions, and vexations the Jews were to suffer after the advent of the Messiah. To justify this interpretation he paraphrases the verse: *"Ipse autem populus direptus et vastatus,"* etc. " They are a people despoiled and trampled under foot," &c., from which words he infers that the Jews have no right to look forward to a Messiah.

IX.—*"If the Jews place their hope of redemption in a future Messiah, and they are still expecting the Messiah, why does the prophet say that the Jews are not to have redemption? For the precise reason, that the Jews expect their salvation from a future Messiah, they must remain without relief; for a new Messiah will never come to the Jews, and as such a Messiah is impossible, so is the relief impossible that the Jews expect therefrom."*

It must be noticed that this prophecy consists of two parts; the first is quoted by the preacher, the second he has taken care to omit. The first represents the troubles, misfortunes, and contumely that Israel suffers in its present dispersion; the second states the good, the greatness, and felicity that Israel will enjoy in its future redemption; and this is given in terms so affectionate and kindly, as to draw tears of joy from every Israelite, still more confirming him in his hopes, and cheering him with a promise of prosperity which he knows cannot fail him.

The following is a translation of the words pronounced by the holy prophet with his accustomed eloquence and inimitable energy of style: "But now, thus saith the Lord, that created thee, O Jacob, and He that formed thee: O Israel! fear not; for I have already redeemed thee, I have called thee by thy name; thou art

mine. When thou passest through the waters
I will be with thee; and through the rivers, they
shall not overwhelm thee; when thou walkest
through the fire, thou shalt not be burned, neither shall the flame kindle upon thee; for I am
the Lord thy God, the Holy One of Israel, thy
Saviour." (Isaiah xliii. 1–3.)

And in the same cheering strain he continues
to the conclusion of the chapter, to comfort and
encourage his beloved Israel, although a sinful,
ungrateful, and rejected people.

I cannot, then, conceive how the preacher can
positively assert, that the prophet declares that
no redemption will come to release Israel from
their present bondage, when he evidently states
the contrary. I wonder that the orator never
contemplated that his sermon might chance to
fall into the hands of some Jew, who, on consulting the passage, chapter xlii., will find that
the preacher has exaggerated the evils therein
threatened, by representing them as irrevocable
and perpetual, whereas the prophet does not protract them beyond the period of the captivity,
also that he suppresses the promised restoration
to prosperity which follows in chapter xliii.

What opinion can that Jew entertain of the
preacher's candor? What conception can he
form of his doctrines? We will still farther develop these important reflections. The preacher
affirms that there will be no redemption for

Israel; but God says, "Fear not, for I have already redeemed thee."

The preacher affirms that God has rejected and discarded Israel from His protection and favor, that He no longer acknowledges them for His peculiar people. God says, "I called thee by thy name, thou art mine." The preacher affirms that Israel, through their manifold iniquities, have lost the glorious privilege they enjoyed when God styled himself the God of Israel. But God says, "I am the Lord thy God, the Holy One of Israel, thy Savior."

I would ask then the preacher, if he can suppose that the Jews will cease to believe the word of God, which is so clear, obvious, and intelligible, in order to attach belief to his own exaggerations, misrepresentations, suppressions of fact, and forced objections? Is he so blind as not to perceive, that the arguments which he advances against their expected Messiah and their long-protracted hopes, are the very same which give them assurance of the one and confirm them in the other; so much so, that the wondering and astonished Israelite will be apt to exclaim, "O God of Truth, are these the proofs that Christians bring against us? Are such preached by their eminent divines, approved of by their most learned prelates, and given to the public press under the highest authorities?"

Blessed art Thou, the great God of Israel, who

hast preserved me in my true faith! for what better proof of its truth can I desire than that of its assailant having no means to confute me save those which spring from disguises, exaggerations, and omissions, contradictions of fact, and quotations so garbled, that I can find the most convincing arguments in its favor in the very passages which he attempts to bring forward to confute it.

XIII.—The preacher says, that if we ask the Jew whether his expected Messiah will be only Man, or both God and Man, he feels greatly perplexed; and on this account the rabbins warned the people, that should such a question be propounded to them, they must reply, that the Messiah has not nor ever will come.

Now, I cannot understand how the Jew can feel any such doubt or embarrassment, while one of the articles of his creed declares that the Messiah is to be a *Man*, and *not God* and *Man*, as will be hereafter shown. I must suppose that this information has been given to the preacher, either by some malevolent neophyte, to gain credit as a good Christian, or by some ignorant Christian, to obtain credit as a deep theologian. If the preacher extracted it from any book, he ought, as is usual, to have stated where he found this famous advice of the rabbins; however, it often happens in controversies, where power and tyranny supersede the necessity of evidence, that the more essential points are admitted without proof; and points of the least importance are dwelt upon and exaggerated.

XIV.—" The Jews are divided in opinion on the advent of the Messiah, some believe that he has not yet appeared, and are still expecting him, whilst others affirm that he came sixteen hundred and thirty-seven years ago, immediately after the destruction of Jerusalem by Titus."

Thus far the preacher in his sermon, although he well knows that no Jew believes, nor ever did believe any such thing, not even the rabbins who speak of the birth of the Messiah, they having represented this imaginary being as if in actual existence, with a view to indicate to the people that the Messiah would be ready to appear at any moment when they should become penitent, as promised by Moses in Deut. iv. 29, where, after intimidating the people with angry threats, he says, that notwithstanding their rebellion, if they seek God with all their heart and with all their soul, they will find Him indulgent and gracious. The same is confirmed in chapter xxx.

Now the rabbins apprehended that the nation, seeing itself dispersed over the three-quarters of the globe, defenceless, without allies or friends, without prince or kingdom, without a temple or sacrifice, and plunged into sad consternation, would give way to a fatal despondency, judging that, having left God and renounced His protection, He had left them exposed to rapine, destruction, and extermination. The rabbins, as vigilant and affectionate parents, endeavored to animate and comfort the people by suggesting, through metaphors, in imitation of the prophets, that their deliverance from the present captivity would be more speedy than what had taken place from Egypt and Babylon, requiring no condition except that of repentance; it being manifested in innumerable passages of the Pentateuch and Prophets, that when the people of Israel should find themselves oppressed with troubles, persecutions, and calamities, on reverting to God with sincere and cordial contrition, they would be redeemed and reinstated in their own land with much greater prerogatives and privileges than those they enjoyed on the two previous occasions; for that, on being finally restored to its possession, they would never again have to apprehend war, hostile invasion, or a renewal of their captivity.

The preacher will perhaps reply, by urging that the rabbins might easily have taught this dogma of the speedy advent of the Messiah, without conjuring up any imaginary being to make the public believe a thing that had no existence. I answer, that they only copied the Prophets, who frequently present figurative descriptions as actual realities. The prophet Isaiah, in his book, chapter v., describes, "A vine planted by his friend in a fertile soil, where he erected a tower and made a wine-press, hoping to gather abundance of choice grapes, but when he gathered them found them only wild in place of cultivated grapes." Here we see a simple allegory, a thing of the imagination, represented by something that had real existence; the prophet himself explaining that by this vine must be understood the house of Israel, from which God expected a nation of pious and devout men, but found them only licentious and dissolute.

Did not God command the prophet Ezekiel to show the people the representation of a great eagle with large wings, expanded limbs, and beautifully variegated plumage, that had broken off the branch of a cedar tree from Lebanon, &c., applying this to Nebuchadnezzar and to the king of Judah?

Thus, then, seeing that God has been pleased to make use of types for the purpose of persuasion, how can the rabbins be blamed when they have done no more than imitate the divine example? But whoever may have informed the lord archbishop, that there are Jews who affirm that the Messiah came immediately after the destruction of the temple, and that the sceptre was lost sixteen hundred and thirty-two years since, must have been very little versed in the belief of the Jews in what concerns the Messiah; since the nation well know that what the rabbins intend by representing the Messiah's birth to have taken place on the destruction of Jerusalem, is merely to signify to the people that the period of redemption is ever at hand; not that his birth has actually and truly occurred, but that it *may* at any moment occur.

How can any Jew believe that the Messiah has come, believing as he does that the purpose of his coming is to collect the dispersed, to deliver them from oppression and persecution, and to place them on the summit of happiness and greatness, rebuilding their city, and restoring it and their temple, and both more sumptuously than they ever were before? Not seeing any particle of all this realized, how can it be imagined that any Jew believes or asserts that the Messiah has already come? Having established this incontrovertible principle, all the remainder of section xiv. becomes of no account; as is also the case with section—

XV.—Wherein it is stated that the modern rabbins affirm that the Messiah has not and will not come, because God has not promised it in the Scriptures, nor is it an article of faith with the Jews. Had the preacher been better versed in the Jewish creed, he would not say this; for the mere assertion that the coming of a Messiah is not an article of his faith would be deemed heresy among the nation. However, Francisco Antonio de Olivares, who adopted this opinion, is only to be blamed for want of information, living as he did in Portugal, where it is not permitted to have or to read any works relative to the Jewish law; moreover, the opinion of an individual is not sufficient to constitute a dogma or form a sect.

Isaiah ix. 5, "*Et vocabitur nomen ejus,*" &c.

In order that the reader may comprehend the real state of the question, it appears to me not only convenient but absolutely requisite to give the verse in dispute in Latin, as well as in the vulgar tongue, and then explain each, that the discerning reader may judge which of the two explanations appears the more correct, more consistent with the literal sense, and more consonant to reason.

The Latin version given by the preacher says: "*Infans natus est nobis, et filius datus est nobis, et erit principatus super humerum ejus, et vocabitur nomen ejus Admirabilis Consiliarius, Deus Fortis, Pater Sempiternus (Pater Sempiternitatis,) Princeps Pax.*"

The translation differs from the Hebrew text. It appears that the preacher, neglecting the promise that he set out with, that his quotations should be always conformable to the original Hebrew, and not to the Vulgate, doubtless believing that there would be no one to contradict him, chooses to forget to have recourse to the former in the present instance; or, to speak more plainly, being well aware that the controversy would be perfectly untenable without some adulteration in the text, had recourse to the Vulgate to help him out in his argument.

In the first instance, he puts the verb *vocabitur* in the future passive, according to which the Hebrew must be read *veyicaré* וְיִקָרֵא which means *he shall be called*. Now, the Hebrew text is *vayicrà* וַיִקְרָא *et vocavit*, which is the preterite active, and must be translated, *and he called*.

Secondly, he puts each of the attributes in the nominative case, applying them all to the Messiah; from which he infers that the Messiah is God, and then calls him a powerful God, Everlasting Father, &c.

Thirdly, he splits up the last attribute into two, turning both the words of which it consists into nominative cases; reading thus *Princeps Pax*, whereas, in the Hebrew, the word *prince* is in the accusative case, governed by the word *vocabit*, and the word *peace* in the genitive, thus making *Principem Pacis*, which means Prince of Peace, not two separate attributes, as the preacher would have; as is evident from the Hebrew, which reads שַׂר שָׁלוֹם *Sar Shalom*, meaning Prince of Peace; the noun שַׂר *Sar* having the (-) *patach* point, indicates the genitive case; whereas, if it constituted an attribute in itself, it should be pointed with a (ׇ) *kametz*. I cannot comprehend then how the preacher so confidently and so readily produces this verse, asserting it to be "conformable to your Hebrew text."

XXIV.—In the twenty-fourth section, he presumes to malign R. Aben Ezra and R. Solomon, who have explained this prophecy of Isaiah, chapter ix. as applying to King Hezekiah, asserting that the former, though convinced from the text that the Messiah was God, yet, out of fear that they might eject him from the Synagogue, affirmed that the passage related to King Hezekiah, and not to the Messiah. According to these assertions of the preacher, Aben Ezra believed the Messiah to be God. Supposing this to be the case, why should he fear being expelled the Synagogue? He might have renounced the Jewish law and gone over to Christianity, where he would have been favorably received, courted, and applauded, being famed as an eminent grammarian, a celebrated astronomer, and an excellent commentator, who kept to the literal sense, and in nowise inclined to allegory, as may be clearly seen in his general commentary on the Bible.

Permit me, reverend father, to inquire by what means your eminence came to the knowledge that R. Aben Ezra became convinced that the Messiah must be God? That you learned it from the rabbi himself is impossible, seeing that he died more than five hundred years ago. The rabbi might have revealed this secret, but to whom could he reveal it? Certainly not to a Jew; for he had to fear the consequences. To a Christian? Not so; for it would have been a stain on the reputation of so learned a man to have professed a religion which he could not defend, and that could not ensure salvation: we cannot, then, imagine by what means the preacher discovered the secret sentiment of this renowned rabbi. Doubtless any Jew, acquainted with the true state of the case, and who is aware that the preacher's intention was merely to inveigle (no matter by what falsehoods) the consciences of his auditors, the pitiable objects of th s Auto da Fé, will in his heart rejoice at perceiving to what arts and inventions he was obliged to have recourse in order to maintain his system.

"Rabbi Solomon, who was esteemed a Solomon among all the Jews, in order to deceive you, professed the same opinion," &c. This horrid calumny was framed in the malevolent brain of the neophyte, Nicholas de Lira, a Norman, on finding himself embarrassed by the "*vocavit nomen ejus.*" (Isaiah, chap. ix.) It surprises me greatly that the Catholic apostolic Roman lord archbishop should avail himself of this calumny, when it is well known that the supreme council of the Inquisition at Rome will not receive any accusation from a neophyte against a Jew. I repeat, it does surprise me that the lord archbishop should admit this ridiculous calumny, when we find (book xv., chapter 13, *De Civitate Dei*) that St. Augustin, one of the principal doctors of the church, affirms it to be incredible that the Jews should have vitiated the sacred books. First, because it appears impossible that they should all have concurred in so vile a purpose, dispersed as they are throughout every part of the world, without finding some one among them to oppose a crime of such enormity, and a sacrilege so abominable as falsifying the sacred text; besides, we find all the Hebrew manuscripts, both ancient and modern, perfectly in accordance with each other in every point: although written at various periods, and in remote regions, indicative of inviolate and accurate fidelity. Neither ought we to presume (continues the same St. Augustin) that so numerous a people, who, in their captivity, have no other property than the possession of the sacred volumes, would consent to falsify them to gratify the malevolence and rancor that they might entertain against any other nation or people: whence he concludes, that where we find a difference between the Hebrew text and the Greek version, most credit ought to be given to the Hebrew, as there is no difficulty in supposing that the Greek interpreter may have committed an error of translation. He termed it a ridiculous calumny, and that justly; it being so

considered and reputed by the whole people of
Israel. Indeed, so scrupulous are they, that if
they perceive in the Book of the Law (which is
read each Sabbath day in the Synagogues) a single
letter more or less than there ought to be, although merely explanatory, and not in the least
altering the sense of the passage or of the words,
that book is immediately laid aside and another
substituted in its place. The rigid notions of the
Jews go still farther in all that relates to the word
of God; for if it should happen that the reader
of the Pentateuch should, either through ignorance or carelessness, mispronounce any word or
accent, that might in any degree alter the meaning, he must repeat the whole of the verse, and,
if not aware of his error, those who hear him
must admonish him, and make him repeat the
verse correctly. This being the practice of the
Synagogues throughout the nation, on discover-
ing any trifling error, written or pronounced,
what would they do if they knew or suspected
that one of the most celebrated rabbins of Israel,
as was R Solomon, had altered the text of Isaiah? Moreover, if our excellent Rabbi Solomon
interprets this prophecy as appertaining to Hezekiah (which really and truly it does, as any one
may see who looks into the Prophecies in order
to understand them, and not to pervert them, as
will be hereafter more fully shown), what necessity was there to alter or corrupt the text? For

admitting it to be as the preacher and the Vulgate pretend, וַיִּקְרָא *veyicarè*, and *vocabitur*, no conclusion can be drawn from this that will militate against the rabbi's exposition; and he might leave the *vocabitur* without exposing himself to the censure of Jew or Christian. R. Solomon, then, having interpreted the prophecy as relating to Hezekiah, and having left the וַיִּקְרָא *vayicrà* and *vocavit* as he found it, it follows that he was not the one who altered and falsified the text, but that this must have been done by St. Jerome, or some one antecedent to him, inasmuch as it appeared to them that the prophecy could not otherwise be explained in the future tense; and by this wretched emendation they hoped to give some show of support to their belief. However, let the preacher know, that the Jews have no necessity for similar acts or frauds to support theirs, inasmuch as, being the word of God, it can maintain and defend itself. If we examine all the *Hebrew* copies, ancient and modern, in any part of the world, we shall find that nothing has been altered, and that they all agree and concur in giving the same simple truth.

The Jew who is conscious of this, will not fail, duly to appreciate the conduct of those, who, not content with vitiating the sacred text themselves, indulge in inventing calumnies as groundless as they are absurd, against the most faithful and excellent expositor that ever lived—a man justly esteemed and venerated by the whole republic of letters, for his commentary on the entire Bible; namely, the Pentateuch, the early and later Prophets, and the Hagiographa, as well as the whole of the Mishnah, and nearly all the Talmud, consisting of sixty-three treatises, arranged in twelve volumes folio, which comprise all the ceremonial, moral, and judicial laws, all of them explained in correct and suitable language, and in a laconic style peculiar to himself, so remarkably clear and intelligible that no one can apply to him, "*Dum arctius esse volo obscurior fio.*"

Perceiving that the vapors of anger were condensing into an opaque cloud, charged with a strong but just resentment against my reckless antagonist, I resolved to repress the warm impulses of my excited feelings, and content myself with laying before him, in the mildest terms, the powerful and irrefragable reasons, which should induce him to retract the charges he has brought against this profound and learned rabbi, who was really a *wise* Solomon, who never deceived (as he asserts), but taught and explained, to all the enlightened nations of Europe, the written and oral laws, which the Jews believe and observe in their dispersion.

The preacher corroborates his hypothesis, or to speak more correctly, he pretends so to do, from the Chaldee version (made by the learned Jonathan, son of Uziel) of the above-mentioned verse of Isaiah, translating it as follows: "*Et vocabitur nomen ejus* Min Kodam, *Deus Fortis, permanens in sæcula sæculorum Messias;*" omitting the end of the verse, which says, "*in cujus diebus multiplicabitur pax.*" Two questions here present themselves, first, why he omitted to translate the expression *Min Kodam?* and the second, why he suppressed the end of the verse?

The reply to these two points will make manifest who it was that corrupted the text, and endeavored to deceive the world.

The inference to be drawn from what I have before stated, bears against the preacher, inasmuch as it proves that he is accustomed to alter, garble, and mutilate the text: while he gives his hearers to understand that he translates literally and faithfully from the Hebrew, saying, "Isaiah has thus written in the ninth chapter of his prophecies, according to your Hebrew text. '*Et vocabitur nomen ejus, Admirabilis, etc. Princeps Pax.*'"

Good Heavens! Has not the preacher just above, accused R. Solomon of having changed the future passive *vocabitur*, "He *shall be* called," into the active form *vocavit*, "*He called;*" thereby rendering the first attributes in the nominative, and leaving the final one (the Prince of Peace) in the accusative case? and here we see him, himself, altering the text, and translating it, not in the least after the Hebrew, but according to his own preconceived notions, just as he has done with the Chaldee paraphrase of Jonathan, son of Uziel, from which he has copied the word *Min Kodam* without translating it, and omitted altogether the last part of the verse, which says, "*In cujus diebus multiplicabitur pax.*"

The true text of Jonathan is as follows:—"*Et vocabitur nomen ejus, a facie, vel ab Admirabili Consiliario, Deo Potente, Patre Æternitatis, Princeps Pacis.*" "And his name shall be called by Him who is the Wonderful Counsellor, Mighty God, and Everlasting Father, *the Prince of Peace* [that is, the Messiah], in whose days peace shall be multiplied."

The first four attributes are of God; the last, "the Prince of Peace, is of man, and in Hebrew, is in the accusative case, being governed by the active verb *vocavit*, and in Chaldee, in the nominative, as in regimen with the passive verb *vocabitur.*"

Min Kodam is a word in the ablative case, omitted by the preacher, because, it did not suit his purpose to insert it; not that *he* was ignorant of its interpretation, since in chap. vii. 11, of the very same prophet, Isaiah says to King Ahaz, "*Pete tibi signum, a facie Domini Dei tui,*" which Montano translates in these words (also taken from Jonathan), "Ask a sign 'from' the Lord thy God." Now, we shall discover the reason why the preacher left *Min Kodam* untranslated; for had he given its meaning, the passage would have run thus: *"Et vocabitur nomen ejus, a facie Admirabilis Consiliarii, Dei Potentes, Patris Æternitatis, Principis Pacis, Messias, in cujus diebus multiplicabitur pax."* "And his name shall be called by the Wonderful Counsellor, the Mighty God, Everlasting Father, Prince of Peace, Messiah, in whose days peace shall be multiplied." According to this rendering, all the attributes belong to the child (as the object called), who is regarded as the Messiah; but then, who is to be taken for the agent, who calls? Whereas, by inserting the words *Min Kodam* (which is the ablative case), the first *four* attributes belong to God, as the agent, who calls; the last one remaining to the child, who is the object *called*. From what has been already said, the discreet and impartial reader will be satisfied that the preacher has altered the text, both in the Hebrew and Chaldee, arranging the words in a way to make it appear that the Messiah was to be both God and Man. But I should wish him to explain why he has taken so much trouble to mutilate and distort these abstruse verses, when after all, if the whole point were conceded, it would amount to no more than an allegory, resting upon a false foundation, and in direct opposition to the primary article of our faith.

It would have been much easier to have laid hold of that article itself (the principal basis of the Jewish religion), which says, "Hear, O Israel, the Lord is our God, the Lord is one," and given the unfortunate prisoners of the tyrannical inquisition to understand that the original text read, "The Lord is *three* and *one*," but that the Jews corrupted it, by omitting two words, so as to be read, "The Lord is *one*." He might have added that Rabbi Solomon, Aben Ezra, and any other rabbi who chanced to enter his mind, was the person who first altered the above-mentioned verse, and that before his time, the Jews accepted the other version; and that the moderns, through their hatred to the Christians, corrupted the text; and here, his excellency might have dilated, displaying his rhetoric in that discursive style so peculiar to himself; by which means, I can assure him, he would have attracted quite as much applause and approbation as he has derived from the arguments which he has employed: nor, need he have feared contradiction from the Christians or the Jews; not from the Christians, for that would not have suited their views; and as for the Jews, they were too illiterate and uninformed; or even were they otherwise, and competent to contradict him, full sure I am that none among them would have dared to lift up their eyes, much less their voices, against *him*. On the contrary, it is certain that their heads would bow assent to whatever he might choose to advance.

Gracious Heaven! how truly absurd must it

M

appear to all impartial persons, when they see a man eminent in his profession, of high rank in the prelacy, disputing with persons who either cannot or dare not answer him, quoting books which they are not allowed to read, and with all this, finds it requisite to distort and mutilate passages of the Holy Scriptures in order to prove what he attempts to inculcate.

I appeal to all learned and unprejudiced men living in countries where they are not constrained to circumscribe their ideas at the will of four illiterate inquisitors, if such a display would not be more fit for a farce than a sermon, for a theatre than a pulpit. They call us blind because we will not yield our reason to groundless allegory; because we do not cede the leading article of our faith to their tortuous and perverted expositions; but what ought they to be called who corrupt the sacred text, who lay hold of part of a chapter, discourse, proposition, or verse, without noticing the context which is necessary to give the genuine sense, in order to apply the fragment as they please, and thereupon raise a shout of victory, as if their opponents had been really and fairly defeated?

Does the learned prelate imagine that this course will convince any Jew? He is deceived if he thinks so; for on the contrary it fortifies him in his belief; and instead of imitating the Inquisition, which prohibits every book that argues against its religion, we publish such works as are written against us, and we explain them to our children, that they may know the truth of *our* reasoning and the fallacy of *theirs;* that they may gain strength in the true belief, and that they may perceive what subterfuge they are driven to who wish to distort the truth, and to what contrivances they must have recourse in order to maintain their opinions.

That the impartial reader may be put in possession of the exact truth relative to the prophecy in question, I will here expound its genuine and literal sense without distortion or allegory, as interpreted by the most eminent and authentic writers:

Commencement of Chapter VII.—Rezin, king of Aram, and Pekah, king of Israel, had laid siege to the holy city of Jerusalem; but, through the gallant resistance of the citizens, were compelled to raise the siege: yet, notwithstanding, they carried off a large booty and a great number of prisoners. The confederated kings formed a new alliance, with the intent of renewing the siege with larger armies and increased vigor. This confederacy threw the house of David into great consternation; for fear that, should those kings conquer, they would put an end to the sovereignty and their kingdom; and the people were no less afraid than the king. Therefore God commanded the prophet Isaiah to go in company with his son, *Shear Yashub,* to meet Ahaz, and to tell him from God to be calm and to comfort his dejected soul, and reanimate his lost spirits, and not to fear these two firebrands, who were more likely to take fire and consume themselves than others: that, although they proposed making a complete conquest of the kingdom, in order subsequently to share it between them, he prophesied to them that such an idea would not be realized; but, on the contrary, Israel (namely, the ten tribes), at the expiration of seventy-five years, would cease to be a nation, would be totally scattered and laid waste, and that in the interim, neither one king nor the other would enlarge the boundary of his dominions, each remaining within his own possessions. God commanded Ahaz, in order to gain confidence in what he had foretold him, to ask for a sign or miracle, whether it be in the highest heaven or in the depths of the earth. The incredulous king excused himself under the pretence of piety, saying that he ought not to require proof from God, whereas the true motive was, the little faith he attached to the words of the prophecy; but the prophet, displeased with his incredulity, said that God would give, although not asked for by the king, a clear and manifest sign, in order to secure the belief of Judea in this prophecy; namely, that the young woman then pregnant should be delivered of a son, who should be named *Immanuel,* and that, before he should attain to years of discretion, the two confederated kings would be totally exterminated. But that, should the stubbornness and perversity of the incredulous king, instead of contritely rendering thanks to God for so signal a deliverance, induce him obstinately to persist in his iniquities, he gave him notice that thereby, Divine justice being in the highest degree provoked, he would inevitably be chastised with greater rigor, by God's allowing the formidable army of the king of Assyria to take possession of all the strongholds and castles of Judea; leaving the land so desolate and uncultivated —so deficient and barren of cattle, that he who possessed one calf and two sheep would be the largest proprietor: and that where, formerly, grew a thousand vines, the ground should become a barren waste, full of thorns and thistles; and the most fertile hills fit only to give pasture to cattle for want of men to cultivate them.

In chapter viii. God commands the prophet to take a scroll, by way of confirming the prophecy, as well as to hand it down to posterity, and write thereon, *Maher-Shalal-Hash-Baz.*

The prophet executed the Divine order, took two witnesses, Uriah and Zechariah, and went unto the prophetess, who conceived and bore a son. He named him (agreeably to the order of God) *Maher-Shalal-Hash-Baz,* intimating, that before this child should learn to call "father" and "mother," the king of Assyria would vanquish in battle the two allied kings, take them captive, and carry away the spoils of Damascus and the riches of Samaria.

However, as there existed a party in Judea who were anxious for the success of Rezin and Pekah, and secretly opposed the reigning family, God ordered the prophet to predict to them, that as they hated the mild and peaceful rule of the house of David, He would bring upon them the formidable armies of the king of Assyria, who should occupy the whole of Judea, until they reached the capital of the kingdom; but that, notwithstanding, He would assist those who were faithful, and deliver them from this peril.

The prophet then reverts to the two allied monarchs, assuring the Jews that all their armaments would not prevail, and that, although they might use their greatest exertion and labor, and increase their forces by the aid of various nations, all would prove ineffectual; and in spite of whatever they might think, their object would never be accomplished. He then proceeds to tell them, that God admonished him to warn them that they should not follow in the steps of those who wished to usurp the government, or who took part with the two allied kings. That he should exhort such persons to defend the just cause, to confide wholly in God, and to fear only the Divine Majesty, who would protect them.— That this prophecy should be sealed and kept close among the learned and wise men until the period of its accomplishment. The prophet also says, although at present God has withdrawn or concealed His protection from us, I trust in His divine mercy, and have full confidence that the desired time will arrive, when it will be clearly manifested, inasmuch as I and my children are obvious signs of what is to happen to Israel; namely, *Yesahya*, the salvation of God; *Shear Yashub*, restoration of the remnant, which indicates that those who remain of Judah shall return to their pristine state; *Maher-Shalal-Hash-Baz*, signifying, that shortly and quickly the prey and spoil of the two kings would follow; *Immanuel*, or God with us; and that when you are required to consult idols and oracles, which always speak vaguely and obscurely, you should answer them that every one must have recourse to his own God, and therefore you should seek to consult the prophets and the professors of the most holy Law. Idols and oracles give unfounded and false answers to those who consult them; and when their votaries find themselves in affliction, assailed by misfortune, hungering and thirsting, they look up to heaven and revile their god for having deceived them with his prophecy, or impute their distress to the bad government of the king; and, finally, when persecuted and harassed with troubles, see nothing before them but vexation and misery, without a gleam of hope of deliverance. Thus it fared with the sons of Zebulun and Napthali in the first captivity; and still worse in the second with those who were carried captive to the East by Tiglath Pilesser, king of Assyria.

In chapter ix. the prophet predicts, that the like shall not occur to the tribe of Judah; for, although they might experience the gloom of a siege and the horrors of war, inasmuch as Sennacherib, king of Assyria, would come against them, still they should receive the light of salvation and the brightness of victory, through the intervention of His divine power, by which the fame of the nation should be exalted to the highest point of glory and greatness; that with indescribable joy and content they should praise and magnify the Eternal and Omnipotent God, in gratitude for so signal and marvellous a deliverance, with all the demonstrations of pleasure evinced by the farmer when gathering in his grain, or the soldier when dividing the spoil.— That the armies of their enemies should be vanquished and annihilated by miraculous aid, and without any of the danger or loss of life which usually befalls the conquerors in a victory attained by natural means; for that the victory would resemble that achieved by Gideon over the Midianites with few men, without loss of life, or even any interference on the part of the conquerors, by the assistance of an angel, who would destroy the hostile army with the same fierceness as fire consumes combustible matter. That this would happen through the merits of that child (already born), on whose shoulders the burden of the monarchy would rest with dignity, and would be named by Him who is the Wonderful Counsellor, Mighty God, the Father of Eternity,—the *Prince of Peace,* (or, if the noble preacher will so have it, let him be called by the name of Wonderful Counsellor, Powerful, Mighty Father of Eternity, Prince of Peace,) who should extend the empire, which should enjoy a perpetual peace, whereby the tottering throne of David would be established on a foundation of justice and charity forever; and that the Lord of Hosts had decreed that all this should come to pass. The prophet proceeds to say, that God having chastised the Ten Tribes of Israel, in order that they might repent and turn away from their sins, the chiefs, with the rest of the people confiding in the alliance of the king of *Aram,* proudly and presumptuously asserted that they were to be restored to a state equal, or even superior, to their former condition; however, God would show them the little worth of that alliance by stirring up Rezin's enemies against him, and giving them power to conquer him in battle, and that afterwards He would so bring it to pass, that these same Aramites on the one hand, and the Philistines on the other, should attack and conquer Israel with great slaughter, without the divine wrath being thereby appeased.

The word *El*, in Hebrew, signifies *strong*, and is an epithet indiscriminately applied to God and man, and when applied to the latter does not signify Divinity, but merely power, greatness, or official station, thus:

אלי מואב, Elé-Moab: princes or valiant men of Moab.

נתתיך אלהים לפרעה, I have made thee superior to Pharaoh.

אשר ירשיען אלהים, whom the judges shall condemn.

Thus, with great propriety, we may apply the title of אל גבור, *El Gibor*, to Hezekiah, indicating thereby that he would be a valiant hero, a great captain; this is confirmed by passages in Scripture, describing him as a man of valor (2 Kings, chapter xx. 20): "And the rest of the acts of Hezekiah, and all his *might*," &c.

The words אבי עד, *Abi 'ad*, which the preacher translates *Pater Æternitatis*, is translated by Montano (in a marginal note), *Pater Seculi*, Father of the Age; to be convinced that this is correct, we need only refer to the Sacred Text.

After the separation of the Ten Tribes from those of Judah and Benjamin, the pious and devout kings of the former, namely, Asa, Jehoshaphat, Jotham, although they anxiously endeavored to establish divine worship in their own kingdom, abstained from interfering with that of Israel, either from its appearing to them impossible to restore it, owing to the contumacy of their kings, or through fear that any communication between Israel and Judah would be likely to infect the latter with their detestable worship of idols. Whereas, Hezekiah, the *father* of the *age*, the common father of both, taking as much care of the strayed sheep that were not under his charge as of those sheltered in his own sheepfold, wrote letters, despatched couriers, and sent qualified persons to all the towns and cities of Israel, exhorting the Israelites to return to the worship of the true God, and to leave the accursed calves; and, with his *wonderful counsel*, managed this great work so admirably as to bring back the alienated Jews to the true worship, as appears from chapter xxx. 1, of the 2d Book of Chronicles: "Hezekiah also sent to all Israel and Judah, and wrote letters to Ephraim and Menasseh, inviting them to come to Jerusalem, to the house of the Lord, to celebrate the Passover of the Lord God of Israel;" and by the same wonderful counsel he transferred the Passover to the second month; thus it is said: "And the king took counsel with his princes and with all the congregation in Jerusalem to celebrate the Passover in the second month." This enabled them all to celebrate it together; and that many of the Israelites actually did come appears from the same Book, chapter xxx. 11: "Moreover, men of the tribes of Asher, Menasseh, and Zebulun humbled themselves and came to Jerusalem;" and in verse eighteen it says: "For many of the people of Ephraim and Menasseh, Issachar and Zebulun had not purified themselves, yet ate of the Passover, contrary to what was commanded; but Hezekiah prayed for them, saying: 'O God! who art benevolent, be merciful to all those who have prepared their hearts to seek thee!'"

It will thus be seen how just a claim he had to the title of *father* of the *age* and *wonderful counsellor*, in having taken so much care to restore them to favor with God. That he was the Prince or Arbiter of Peace, there can be no doubt. For what person in that age would venture to oppose Almighty God, who, by so many prodigies, had proclaimed himself the protector of Hezekiah; since He sent an angel to be the commander of his armies, a prophet to heal his diseases, and ordered the sun to retrograde in its diurnal course in order to confirm his prophecies by this marvelous event, which caused Baladan, king of Babylon, to send ambassadors to inquire into this miracle, and to seek his alliance?

From the above-mentioned chapters, translated literally, and applied to the actual persons of whom they treat, we find that the sign the prophet gave to Ahaz was, that the young woman had conceived, and that she would give birth to a son who should be called Immanuel. The prophet had taken two faithful witnesses to record, namely, Uriah and Zechariah; and succeeding events were found to be in perfect accordance with the prophecy. The prophet went to the young woman, who was his wife; she conceived and gave birth to a son: him they named Immanuel, and before he had arrived at years of discretion the designs of the two allied monarchs were rendered abortive.

Such then is the literal exposition of this prophecy; and to attempt to dispute it would be only arguing in opposition to facts. Indeed, such an attempt, in the eyes of those who have studied the Scriptures free from all bias, must appear a virtual acknowledgment of defeat, and a mere display of weakness. Moreover, this miracle or sign was given to Ahaz and the house of David, in order to certify to them that the kings of Samaria and Aram would not follow up their intentions, and that their designs would be frustrated. How then could a sign be given to them to indicate what was to happen in the course of about seven hundred years, in order to show what was to occur within *two* or *three years?* and how could the prophet say (from an event which was to occur about seven hundred years subsequently), "It shall come to pass, that before the child shall know to distinguish between bad and good, the land you hate shall be bereft of its two kings?" Are not these two kings Rezin, king of Aram, and Pekah, king of Israel? And is it not clearly meant that they should both be defeated and conquered in battle, and should lose their kingdoms? How, then, to assure them of what was to occur in their lifetime, could he give them a sign from what was to happen seven hundred years later, and this to an incredulous and idolatrous king like Ahaz: would it not have exposed the prophet to the derision of the king and his court? Most assuredly it would; and the learned among the Christians, who study this prophecy impartially, are not ignorant of this, and consequently agree that such is the true, literal, and genuine sense, as confessed by Eusebius Basilius, Geronimus Cirilius, and Theodoretus, among the ancients; and there are but few among the well informed moderns who do not acquiesce therein, and admit that even the allegorical sense is not solely applicable to Christ, but might equally be adapted to any other person, without perverting or straining the text: whence we see that those erudite and wise men know that the allegorical sense is not compulsory, and therefore is insufficient to constrain the Jews to admit it. All are agreed that the prophecy explained literally is clear and obvious, and not in the least degree perplexed or obscure; and that it was fulfilled a few years afterwards, as the prophet predicted, to the very letter.

But this is not the case when we attempt to apply it in an allegorical sense to Christ; for it then becomes obscure, confused, and inappropriate, and compels us to resort to the corrupt text of the Vulgate to render it applicable, and even *that* will not be found sufficient.

I flatter myself that I have placed this prophecy in such a light as to show my co-religionists (as is the purport and scope of my refutation) how little reason the learned preacher has to exult over this passage: and he could only do so among those whose ignorance rendered them unable to discern the truth, or whose dread of punishment prevented their proclaiming it.

The preacher, in confirmation of his hypothesis, refers to chapters xxiii. and xxxiii. of Jeremiah, gives the verses five and six of chapter xxiii., and attempts to explain them after his own views, as alluding to the Messiah; stating that the prophet says, "That a just king will come," &c., and "*that king* will be called *Deus justus noster.*" However, he takes no farther notice of chapter xxxiii.; and, deeming his bare assertion sufficient, unhesitatingly affirms that, from the verses of these two chapters, it is evident that the Messiah must be God and man. I am not surprised at his omitting verses fifteen and sixteen of chapter xxxiii.; for he has done a similar thing in the sixth paragraph, wherein he quotes from chapter xlii. of Isaiah, in which God threatens his people with chastisement and calamities, and omits the forty-third, that immediately follows, wherein He encourages and consoles them with affection and tenderness. Let us examine, then, these two verses, by which means we may penetrate into the true cause of this omission: *"In Diebus illis salvabitur Juda, et Jerusalem habitabit confidenter, et hoc est nomen vocabunt eum, Dominus Justus noster."* I know not to what we are to refer this *eum* masculine, when the Hebrew says לה (*lah*), a pronoun feminine, which can only refer to the city of Jerusalem; this being indubitably the case, the verse must mean *Jerusalem* shall be called "God is our right or justice:" this same word is applied to the Messiah in chapter xxiii. Now, as the preacher says that, since he is so called, he must be both *God* and *Man*, it would follow that Jerusalem, bearing a similar name, is at the same time God and City. The like I say of the altar erected by the patriarch Jacob in *Shechem* (Genesis, chap. xxxiii. 20). The like of that erected by Moses for the victory obtained over Amalek, which he called "God is my standard." The same with the altar of Gideon, which he called "God of peace;" and, finally, the same with Jerusalem, when the prophet Ezekiel, in the last verse of his book, says, that Jerusalem will be called "God is there."—Now, to conclude my observations on this point, the reverend preacher should be told, that the hymn he names, which is chaunted in the Synagogue on every Sabbath and Holiday evening, is, in fact, a declaration of the articles of the Law which the Jews profess, and that the third of the said articles declares that God is incorporeal, and consequently is *not Man*, which article of the creed is derived from various parts of the Bible. Moses says, addressing the people (Deut. chap. iv. 12): "And God spoke to you from amidst the fire; you heard a voice speaking, but you saw no similitude, only a voice;" and farther says (Deut. chap. iv. 15), "Take good heed to yourselves; for ye saw no similitude on the day that God spoke to you out of the midst of the fire;" and continues, charging them strenuously not to make a likeness of any manner of creature. Balaam, although a gentile, says: "*God* is *not Man* that he should lie, nor the *Son of Man* that he should repent.*"* The holy prophet Samuel said to King Saul: "Surely, the Strength of Israel will not lie, nor repent; for he is *not Man* that he should repent." "*Et etiam fortitudo Israelis non mentietur nec pœnitudine ducetur ; non enim homo est ut pœniteat illum.*"

Ezekiel said to Hiram, king of Tyre, who boasted of being a god: "Perchance thou mayest venture to say before the assassin, I am God; then thou shalt be made to know that thou art but man, not a god, when in the power of thy murderer." "*Nunquid dicendo Deus sum, coram interfectore tuo; tu autem Homo es, et non Deus, in manu interfectoris tui:"* finally, God says through His prophet: "I will not, according to the fury of my wrath, I will not again do injury to Ephraim; for I am God, and not Man." *"Non faciam secundum iram furoris mei, non revertar ad disperdendum Ephraim, quoniam Deus sum et non Vir."*

These are the pillars on which this most important article, the immateriality of God, rests; which, if any Jew should deny, he would not only be considered a heretic, but a renegade, and forfeit among his people all claim to the denomination of Jew: can it then be imagined that the nation will cease to believe an article so clear, and so frequently reiterated by the prophets, to follow the exposition contended for by the reverend father?

Thus the honor of the learned Rabbi Solomon stands vindicated and cleared from the vile calumny of having falsified the words of the prophets; and sufficient proof has been given that, as a Jewish theologian, he could not believe or imagine that chapter ix. of Isaiah, and chapters xxiii. and xxxiii. of Jeremiah declare that the Messiah must be *Man* and *God*.

The same remark will apply to the eminent Rabbi Aben Ezra; to Jonathan, the son of Uziel, and, finally, to every son of Israel, no matter how uninstructed or ignorant. However this may be, I cannot but express my astonishment that the preacher, who endeavors to make it appear that Jonathan, the son of Uziel, infers from the words (in chapter ix. of Isaiah, ver. 6), "*Infans natus est*," that the Messiah is God, does not avail himself of his authority and countenance in chapter xxiii. and xxxiii. of Jeremiah, but uses the Hebrew text alone, without adverting to the Chaldee paraphrase; and that he should exercise his ingenuity in again calumniating the innocent but persecuted Rabbi Solomon, charging him with having falsified the text in chapter xxiii. of Jeremiah, and venture to assert that the true reading gives: "And this is the name that *they* shall call him," not "that *He* shall call him," which latter he treats as a corruption introduced by the rabbi; and that he should quote the text of chapter xxiii., where he makes the prophet declare that the Messiah is God, and omits to quote from chapter xxxiii., where precisely the same language is applied to the city of Jerusalem.

What reply can he make to this? that he does not pretend to say that the city of Jerusalem is God. Granted; but why, then, does he set up a general axiom, affirming that the Tetragrammaton is applied to none other but God, when, in fact, we find it applied to inanimate objects, such as altars and cities? Agreeably to his axiom, all these things must be gods; he may endeavor to solve the difficulty by saying that man, as the most noble of all creatures, was alone capable and worthy of being united with the Deity; to this I answer, I only know that God has declared, by the mouth of His prophet Hosea, "I am God and not Man," and I need say no more.

XXV. and XXVI.—The preacher goes on to say, that the rabbins explain the prophecy in chapter ix. of Isaiah as relating to Hezekiah, and in chapters xxiii. and xxxiii. of Jeremiah, to David and Zerubabel. As regards Isaiah, the preacher is correct in affirming that the rabbins apply the passage to Hezekiah, and I am of the same opinion, as may be seen by the exposition of the prophecy above given, where I have shown that the first verses of chapter ix. treat of nothing else but the miraculous triumph that Israel gained over Sennacherib; according to such view, the two parts of the chapter agree in alluding to one and the same event; and there is no occasion to interpret it as referring to the Messiah, who is sufficiently spoken of in many other passages of the Bible. As to the two chapters of Jeremiah, I know no rabbi who thinks they allude to any one else but the Messiah.

The preacher bestows needless labor in attempting to prove that Rabbi Solomon has falsified the text, and in ridiculing the exaggeration of the writers, who relate of the eminent Jonathan, that a fly passing over any of his writings was instantly consumed. Had the preacher reflected that the rabbinical style is frequently figurative, he would have perceived that the above cited metaphorical passage merely implied that this great man was so studious and attentive during his meditations on the Law, that, should any worldly thought intrude on his mind while so engaged, it was instantly subdued and annihilated.

XXVII.—The reverend preacher takes great pains to prove that the passage in chapter ix. of Isaiah speaks of the Messiah; and to this end brings forward a host of rabbins, ancient and modern, as of that opinion. Although we have had sufficient evidence already of how little weight can be attached to the preacher's pretended proofs, I am willing, for the sake of argument, to waive my objections, and will be liberal enough to invite all Israel to take it for granted, as he says; for, after all, the principal question (*summa rerum*) is to ascertain if the Messiah truly is God.

XXXIII.—Our author alleges that the rabbins, finding themselves in difficulty on points proposed to them, could find no means to extricate themselves, except by vitiating the text; but they had no necessity to vitiate the text, since we see that the aforementioned article of their creed directly forbids any Jew to believe that God can be also *man*.

XXXIV.—XXXIX.—These are answered by the aforementioned article of belief. In the 23d chapter, we grant that Jeremiah speaks of the Messiah; but not that he says, nor that it can possibly be inferred from his words, that the Messiah is God.

XLI.—Two rabbins are herein named, viz: R. Osseas and R. Simeon ben Jochay. Rabbi Osseas never appeared *in rerum natura*. There is not and never was a rabbi of that name. The other, who he affirms flourished many years before Christ, was not in existence till more than a century after, and in no book attributed to him do we find what the preacher has stated; and farther, were such an opinion to appear in any book that has come down to us (which we absolutely deny), that rabbi would be condemned as a renegade, and his doctrine would carry with it no weight whatever.

XLII.—The same reply may be made to this section, namely, that whoever believes or writes that the Messiah is God and Man, is no Jew; that is to say, he does not profess the Law of Moses, consequently his doctrine cannot influence us as Jews. Towards the end of this same section, the observation made in the sixth is repeated, and a quotation given from chapter xlii. ver. 22 of Isaiah, "*Ipse autem populus direptus et vastatus.*" In addition to what I have already remarked upon this passage, I refer the reader to chapter xliii., which annihilates all that the preacher advances; for it states clearly that Israel is God's people, and that redemption is assured to them in accordance with the statements in the preceding chapter.

XLIII. and XLIV.—The reverend father boasts, with much confidence, of having convinced the Jews by chapter xlix. verse 10 of Genesis, *"Non auferetur sceptrum à Juda, nec scriba de femore ejus donec veniat Shilo (vel qui mittendus est) et ipse aggregatio populorum."* But he should be informed that he is much deceived in his conception of this prophecy. It must be kept in mind, that the name Judah represents four very different objects, and is capable of as many different acceptations, as is taught in the schools.

It may be received for Judah, the son of Jacob, as in this same chapter (Genesis xlix. ver. 8), where it is said: "Judah, thou art he whom thy brethren shall praise, the sons of thy father shall bow down to thee."

It may be received solely for the tribe of Judah, as in verse ten of the abovementioned chapter, where it is said: "The sceptre shall not depart from Judah." Again, it may be taken for the two tribes, Judah and Benjamin; because, subsequently to the separation of the Ten Tribes, all the kings who reigned over the two are *called* kings of Judah, as tacitly comprising that of Benjamin; finally, it may be taken for the Twelve Tribes, which form the whole body of Israel, as in Jeremiah, chap. xxxiii. ver. 11, where, speaking of the Messiah, it says: "In those days Judah shall be saved, and Jerusalem shall be inhabited in safety." Here, evidently, the name of Judah is used to denote *all* Israel.

This incontrovertible principle being established, we are compelled to receive the name of Judah in verse ten, where it says: "That the sceptre shall not depart from Judah," as meaning neither the individual nor the whole nation, but the single tribe. Not the individual; for we cannot suppose that the patriarch understood that his son Judah would live and reign until the Messiah came, or that the verse really meant that the sceptre should not depart from Judah *himself* until the Messiah came. Nor was it meant to express the whole nation; for, as Jacob was blessing his sons, each separately, one by one, it is evident that he is addressing himself to Judah *individually*, and prophesies to him in the words: "*Non auferetur sceptrum à Juda,*" that the sceptre shall remain permanently in his tribe without ever passing into the hands of any of the others; accordingly, the preacher cannot plead in argument against the Jews that the sceptre departed from the nation on the birth of Christ, who, in his opinion, was the Messiah, inasmuch as the sceptre of Judah had failed many years antecedently in king Zedekiah, without ever returning to Judah; and, this being indisputably the case, it follows necessarily that the prophecy is either false, or wrongly explained. In order to obviate these difficulties, it must be observed that, by understanding this prophecy in a literal sense, as in reason we ought to do, we shall perceive that it contains no allusion to the Messiah, nor to any period later than the epoch of the separation of the kingdoms of Israel and Judah; much less does it treat of the tribes as members of the body of the nation, excepting in one instance, and that indirectly and incidentally. That it does not treat of the Messiah is fully proved by the circumstance related in Scripture, that the holy patriarch having assembled his sons, proceeded to describe to them what was to happen at the end of days. (Genesis, chapter xlix. ver 1.) It might appear at first sight, from this passage, as if he intended to make some allusion to the Messiah, always supposing that the expression, *the end of days,* is to be understood as denoting the period of the Messiah, in accordance with chapter ii. ver 2 of Isaiah, where the prophet, describing the supreme felicity of that epoch, says: "And it shall come to pass at the *end of days,* or in the latter days, that the mountain of the Lord's house shall be established on the summit the mountains," &c.

This prophecy we find confirmed in Micah, chapter iv. ver. 1, in precisely the same words. The prophet Jeremiah also makes use of the same terms, when describing the prosperity of

Israel at the epoch of the Messiah, in chapter xxx. ver. 24, and the prophet Ezekiel in chapter xxxviii. ver. 16.

The holy patriarch then having used the same words, it might naturally enough, at first sight, be supposed he was speaking of the Messiah, as before remarked; but, when we come to investigate more closely what he said on that occasion, we shall find that he neither alluded to the Messiah, nor to the people of Israel in general. This is clearly evinced by what he said to his sons; since, as to Reuben, he only reproved him for his conduct with Bilhà, also Simeon and Levi for their rash conduct towards Shechem on account of Dinah, (Judah we shall notice immediately.) To Zebulun he predicted that the territory allotted to him would be maritime. To Asher, that his country would be fertile and pleasant; and, in short, there is nothing said about the Messiah.

It is true that all Christian commentators, and many of the Jews explain the words: *"Non auferetur sceptrum à Juda;"* "The sceptre shall not depart from Judah," &c., figuratively, as relating to the Messiah; however, the literal translators among the Jews only understand it to indicate the separation of the kingdom of Israel from that of Judah, interpreting the prophecy in the following manner: "Thee, Judah, thy brethren will praise, and bow down to thee; for thou art intrepid as a lion, and supremacy will be conceded to thee. The rule thou possessest over the whole nation will continue undivided until the Shilonite shall come, who will separate the Ten Tribes from the two others; and then to *him*, that is to say, to Judah, it will be left to gather together certain people, meaning the two tribes of Judah and Benjamin, with the priests and Levites dispersed throughout all Israel, who will quit their glebe-land, habitations, and property, and assemble in Jerusalem, as well as many other pious Israelites, who, imitating the priests and Levites, will fix their residence in the country of Judah, in order not to abandon the holy and divine worship professed by their pious and devout ancestors."

That such is the genuine and literal sense of the prophecy concerning Judah there can be no doubt, from the numerous reasons that support this exposition, and from the many irrefragable objections that arise against a figurative explanation, as we shall proceed to prove.

The first objection is, that the allegorists seek by violently torturing the word *Shiloh* to make it imply the Messiah, when, in fact, it is the name of a famed city in the Holy Land, wherein the Ark of God reposed during three hundred and sixty-nine years, having been placed there by Joshua, as may be seen in chapter xviii. verse 1 of the Book of Joshua, in which it is named seven times; in Judges, six; in the first book of Samuel, eight times; in the first book of Kings, twice; in Jeremiah, four times; in Psalms, once; thus making twenty-eight times in all that it has been named in the Bible. The prophet Ahijah, the Shilonite, is named in 1 Kings, chapters xi., xii., and xiv., proving clearly and literally that Shiloh was the name of a city, and the prophet Ahijah a native of that city; I know not, then, what could induce the allegorists to construe the name of a city so well known in a sense so remote from its true signification. The second objection, which appears unanswerable, militates against Jonathan son of Uziel, and Onkelos, for having framed an allegory on a principle that has not only been contested, but is actually contradicted by the evidence of facts, affirming, as they do, that the sceptre would not fail Judah until the advent of the Messiah, whereas they must have known that it did fail in the Babylonian captivity,— and that the nation, after being re-established in Judea, and living under subjection to the Persians and Greeks, at length succeeded in breaking and throwing off the heavy and cruel yoke of the latter, and took for themselves kings from the tribe of Levi, and *not* from that of Judah,—and, when these became extinct, they chose Herod and his descendants for their kings, until nearly the end of the second temple, when the sceptre, that is, what little power had remained in the nation, ceased altogether until the present time.

In proceeding to investigate this formidable objection, we are first compelled to suppose that two eminent sages like these could not be so rash as to frame an allegory so contradictory to the literal sense; for, if what the allegory represents be true, what the patriarch says must be false, as proved by the preceding quotations. Next it becomes necessary to explain the allegory in a manner not only that it may be seen not to contradict the prophecy, but that it may indicate something of the same tendency.

The learned, both Jews and Christians, ever prefer the literal sense to the figurative. The rabbins clearly say, in the Treatise on the Sabbath, chapter v., that "the Sacred Text can never be diverted from its literal signification;" and Cornelio a Lepide, in his Canons on the Pentateuch, Can. 40, says: *"In sensu literali omnis sententiæ omniaque verba debent explicare et accommodari rei significatæ, id autem non est necesse in sensu allegorico."* Allowing this, we find that, according to the paraphrases of Jonathan and Onkelos, the literal sense of the patriarch's prophecy is contrary to, and incompatible with the allegorical interpretation; for, agreeably to that, from the time King David held the sceptre, the sovereignty should never have failed from the house of David, which is the same thing as to say from

o*

the tribe of Judah. *"Sed sic est,"* that it did fail in Zedekiah, the last king, at the destruction of Jerusalem, without ever returning to that tribe, as was seen in the second temple; *ergo*, conformably to the allegory of these sages, we are constrained to say, either that the patriarch's prophecy was false (which would be an odious heresy and horrid blasphemy), or that the two allegorists knew not how to adapt the allegorical to the literal sense; this would be a paradox, as the interpretation given by them of many passages in the Bible, that would otherwise have appeared to us incomprehensible, clearly evinces the knowledge and capabilities of these most eminent sages. The difficulty is greatly enhanced on seeing that, since the destruction of the second temple, till the present time, the sceptre has failed in Israel; how, then, can we ever reconcile the allegory with the prophecy, since the allegory confidently affirms that the sceptre will never fail in Judah, whereas the prophecy neither promises nor indicates any such thing? The only mode I can see of solving this formidable difficulty, is to draw a distinction between possession and jurisdiction, and to understand the text conformably to the allegorists, as representing the patriarch to speak of *jurisdiction*, not of actual *possession*, which will serve to make the sense of the prophecy clear.

"Judah (said the holy patriarch), thy brethren

will cede the superiority to thee, thy father's
children will bow down to thee, for thou art intrepid, and bold as a lion." If, in any time, Judah
should forfeit the crown, and the sceptre pass into
another tribe, the patriarch assures him that he
has nothing to fear, for what he had lost would
be merely the possession for a limited time; the
jurisdiction always remaining intact and reserv-
ed, to be enjoyed as a perpetual possession in the
person of the future Messiah.

Nevertheless, as the greater number of commentators are ever inclined to view the phrase,
"*Non auferetur sceptrum à Juda*," as a prophecy
assuring this tribe of a continued and uninterrupted empire until the coming of the Messiah,
I find it requisite to invalidate this opinion, and
to prove, from various passages and prophecies
in the Holy Bible, that God had many times
threatened his incorrigible people with the down-
fall of their crown and destruction of their kingdom.

In Leviticus, chapter xxvi. ver. 33, God says:
"I will scatter you among the nations, and draw
out a sword after you, and your land shall be desolate, and your cities waste."

Here we read of dispersion, desolation of the
land, and the destruction of cities. Things incompatible with the crown and sceptre.

In Deuteronomy, chapter iv. ver. 27, we read,
"And the Lord shall disperse you among the

nations, and ye shall be left few in number among the heathen, whither the Lord shall lead you."

In chapter xxviii. ver. 36, Moses says: "The Lord will bring thee, and thy king whom thou wilt set over thee, unto a nation which neither thou nor thy fathers have known."

From these texts in the Pentateuch may clearly be inferred the total destruction of the kingdom, and the complete dispersion of the nation. I, therefore, cannot perceive whence is derived this boasted certainty of the permanency of the kingdom of Judah till the advent of the Messiah. I am aware I shall be told that this promise is made perfectly obvious and clear in 2 Samuel, chapter vii. verses 15 and 16, where God says to David, speaking of his son Solomon, "But my mercy shall not depart from him, as I took it from Saul, whom I put away before thee; and thine house and thy kingdom shall be established forever before thee: thy throne shall be established forever."

In 1 Kings, chapter ix. ver. 3, to the 11th inclusive, in a vision that appeared to Solomon, after having dedicated the temple, God said to him, that He had accepted his dedication, and that His name, His eyes, and His heart, would attend on that house perpetually, and that, if he would follow the steps of David his father, serving Him with a perfect and upright heart, and observe His precepts, that He would establish his throne perpetually over Israel, as He had promised to His servant David, saying, "There shall not fail thee a man upon the throne of Israel; but if you should turn from following me, yourself, or your children, and will not keep my commandments and my statutes, which I have set before you, but go and serve other gods, and worship them: then will I cut off Israel out of the land which I have given them; and this house, which I have hallowed for the sake of my name, will I cast out of my sight, and Israel shall be a proverb and a byword among all people; and at this house, which is now so high, every one that passeth by it shall be astonished, and shall hiss, and exclaim, Why hath the Lord done this unto this land and to this house? And the reply shall be, Because they forsook the Lord their God, who brought forth their fathers out of the land of Egypt, and they resorted to other gods, and they worshipped them and served them; therefore hath the Lord brought upon them all this evil."

This revelation and promise explain what God would do for David, from which we may incontestably infer, that the greatness, the happiness, and the perpetuity of the sovereignty which God promised David and Solomon, were only *conditional*, and not absolute. Although *secundum alegata et probata*, my hypothesis is already firmly established, to the effect that God never did promise the patriarch Jacob, or king David, or king Solomon, his son, the perpetuity of the crown (at least until the advent of the Messiah), I will, by way of putting the question forever at rest, proceed to show, that so far from such promise having ever been made, God revealed to David the profanation of the temple, the destruction of Jerusalem, and the cruel massacre of the people; all which David bitterly bewails in Psalm lxxix., wherein he says: "O Lord! the heathen are come into thine inheritance; thy holy temple have they defiled: they have laid Jerusalem in heaps; the dead bodies of thy servants have they given to be meat to the fowls of heaven; the flesh of thy saints unto the beasts of the earth! Their blood have they shed like water round about Jerusalem, and there was none to bury them." The remainder of the Psalm is filled with lamentation over the calamities of the nation.— This Psalm was either composed by Assaph, the Levite, a musician of the holy house, and dedicated to David, or may have been composed by David himself, and dedicated to Assaph, as may be inferred from chapter xxv. of 1st Chronicles: and as all the Psalms were of divine inspiration, we must conclude that God chose to reveal to David the future destruction of Jerusalem; nor will it avail to say, that David speaks of his own time, deploring the loss of some battle, the result of which constituted the misery that the Psalmist describes. It will not avail, I say, to use a frivolous subterfuge, it being obvious to us, that David never had a battle but wherein he was victorious; and it is a notorious fact, that the gentiles never did, in his time, either enter Jerusalem, defile the temple, or demolish the holy city; and that the massacre described in the Psalm never took place. *Ergo*, this must have been a prophetic revelation to David or to Assaph, whence it may be deduced that David knew that God's promise of perpetuity of the sovereignty in his family was *conditional*, not *absolute*.

To silence criticism effectually, and leave no room for contradiction, it will be sufficient merely to read Psalm cxxxii. 11, 12, where it says, "The Lord hath sworn in truth unto David, he will not turn from it, Of the fruit of thy body will I set upon thy throne. If thy children will keep my covenant and my testimony that I shall teach them, their children shall sit upon thy throne for evermore."

From these verses we see that David himself acknowledges that the perpetuity of the kingdom and his family, previous to the coming of the Messiah, was to be *conditional*, and *not absolute*. We might also quote the Psalm cxxxvii. which represents the people as captives in Babylon; but there being no title attached to this Psalm, and there being many who suppose it to have been composed in Babylon by some feeling and pious person (although such is not my opinion), I will not make use of it, more especially as I consider that the arguments already adduced have established my hypothesis on an indestructible foundation.

XLV. and LII.—In order to prove his assumption, the preacher recurs to the statue in Nebuchadnezzar's dream, interpreting the three first metals, gold, silver, and copper, to mean the three monarchies, Chaldean, Persian, and Greek, and applies the fourth, iron, to Roman, ascribing the potter's clay to the Jewish kingdom, which was not united with the iron, but mixed with it,—mixed, that is to say, by the alliance that existed between the Romans and the Jews, by virtue of which the Romans were obliged, in case of war, to succor and defend them. He then adds, that the stone without hands, that struck the statue and reduced it to powder forever, scattered and destroyed the clay, together with the four metals.

I would ask the Lord Archbishop, supposing that Israel is doomed to remain permanently scattered and destroyed, what necessity would there be for the Messiah? and for whom need he to come? who would there be to enjoy the promised greatness and happiness during the period of his reign? How would the prophecy be accomplished that Jeremiah proclaims (chap. xxiii.

5), "Behold, the days come, saith the Lord, that I will raise unto David a righteous Branch, and a just king shall reign and prosper, and shall do justice and charity in the land; in his days shall Judah be saved, and Israel shall dwell in *safety*," &c.?

The same is confirmed in chap. xxxiii., ver. 15 and 16, and also in ver. 17, where it says, "Thus saith the Lord, There shall not be cut off from David a man to sit on the throne of the house of Israel." · Now if the destruction of Israel had been typified by the crumbling of the clay of the colossus, according to the hypothesis of the archbishop, over whom is this just and charitable king to reign? Who are the people that are to enjoy his mild dominion? What nation will have the merit to attain the favor of his protection?

It is a dangerous experiment, by means of any such ill-explained and misapplied allegories, to attempt to convince the nation among whom it has never been the practice to swerve from the literal sense of Holy Writ, and that with good reason and justice, as the literal word of God is pure, clear, unalterable, inviolable, and incontrovertible, whilst allegory is merely a frail human invention, frequently inapplicable, and when applicable, oftener conducing to error than to truth.

Besides the incontestable proofs quoted from the prophet Jeremiah, an infinite number more might be collected from all the prophets; however, I shall confine myself solely to confuting the false proposition which the preacher ventures to advance (namely, that the breaking in pieces of the clay of the statue, is to be interpreted as applicable to Israel), and endeavor to convince him by the words of the prophet Daniel, chapter ii. ver. 44. "*Porro tempore regum istorum suscitavit Deus cœli regnum quod in æternum non corrumpitur, et regnum istud populo alteri non relinqueter; comminuet et consumat omnia ista regna, et ipsum stabit in æternum!*"

"But in the days of these kings the God of Heaven will raise up a kingdom that will never be destroyed, and the kingdom shall not be surrendered to any other people; but it shall break in pieces and consume all these kingdoms, and *it* shall stand forever!"

The toes, partly of iron, and partly of clay, indicate that a portion of the kingdom should remain firm, and the rest be broken up. It cannot be inferred that there are two kingdoms, as the preacher imagines; but merely, that there is *one* kingdom, part of which will be strong, and the other part weak. *Ergo*, he cannot affirm that the clay is a fifth kingdom, indicating the Jewish empire.

XLVIII.—Our author proceeds with much confidence to assert, that the prophet foretells that the advent of the Messiah would take place while the Roman empire and the Jews were still mingled together; and that, on his coming, he would destroy in the Jews the clay of their kingdom, and in the Romans the iron of their empire; for from the ruins of these two dominions would arise the kingdom of the Messiah, which, &c.

From this, he brings to bear against the Jews a dilemma, which appears to him to be irrefutable, alleging that the Roman empire is no longer mingled with the kingdom of the Jews; nor is the kingdom of the Jews mingled with that empire, for that both these powers are destroyed; and goes on to say, that the kingdom of Christ is now spread all over the world, and denies that the Messiah can come after that destruction, but that the destruction was to *follow* his coming. So formidable does the preacher consider this dilemma, that he persuades himself the Jews will remain convinced and confuted, without having a word to say in reply; but he does not consider what has been stated and proved above, namely, that in this colossal statue there was no substance whatever that indicated the Jews. This having been already clearly established, we see the chimerical invention of the preacher's dilemma, as completely fallen, demolished, and crumbled into dust, as the statue of Nebuchadnezzar itself.

To confirm this fact, it will be sufficient merely to read the beginning of Daniel chapter vii., where he relates seeing, in a vision, the same four monarchies, which Nebuchadnezzar had seen represented by the four metals, gold, silver, copper, and iron, depicted to him under the type of four wild beasts,—a lion, a bear, a tiger, and another, whose figure he only describes as monstrous, hideous, and most dreadful in form and aspect.

If then this vision of Daniel was the counterpart of that of Nebuchadnezzar, with this single difference, that the emblems in the one case consisted of metals, and in the other of animals, it follows, that, as in Daniel's we count only four animals, representing the four monarchies, so in Nebuchadnezzar's the number must also be four.

To convince the Jews by means of allegories, is as futile as to attempt retaining water in a sieve; for the Hebrew nation never abandons the literal sense of the Scriptures; concluding, and with reason, that the literal sense is the true word of God, pure, sincere, inviolable, and infallible, while allegory is nothing more than a conjecture, an idea, a presumption, a chimera, concocted from the slender materials that the circumscribed knowledge of the human mind can supply.

The preacher explains the metals in Nebuchadnezzar's statue, according to the principles which he considers suited to his own purpose, and, contrary to the fact, represents the Roman empire as already destroyed. To see this more clearly, it must be noticed, that the Persians, who conquered the Babylonian monarchy, destroyed and annihilated it in a manner that it remained *extra rerum naturam*, as we learn from the sacred Scriptures, and from the history of those times, which explains the statue's remaining without the head of gold. The Persian monarchy was subverted and demolished by the Greeks, that of the Greeks, by the Romans; thus three metals are disposed of, and there only remains the iron, mixed with the clay. This indicates the Roman empire, which subsists and remains, down to the present day. True, it is not with so extended a territory, or wide a jurisdiction, as in former times, but still incontrovertibly as the same Roman empire, although confined within very narrow limits; for the emperor of Germany, before being crowned emperor, takes up the title, in his father's life, of king of the Romans, and after becoming emperor, enjoys the same titles and dignities as his ancestors, he being called Cæsar and Augustus; and, as such, a pre-eminence is conceded to him by all the kings and potentates of Europe, without dispute or opposition.

If the feet of iron, which represent the Roman empire, remain, it involves a contradiction, to suppose that the stone now fills the earth with its bulk; for the prophet says, that the stone, after having reduced all the metals to dust, was converted into an immense mountain, that filled the whole earth: now, allowing that the fourth metal still subsists, there can be no stone, for they cannot exist together; "*Sed sic est*," that the metal does exist; *ergo*, the stone cannot yet have appeared, and consequently the Messiah is not yet come.

To establish the doctrine of the Messiah's having already come, our author avails himself of the pretended authority of the Talmudic rabbins, whom he quotes as affirming that the final ם (*Mem*) contained in the word לםרבה (*lemarbè*) Isaiah, chapter ix. verse 7, which numerically represents *six hundred*, indicates that so many years had passed from the promulgation of that prophecy to the death of Christ; and that it had always been held, that when those six hundred years were expired, the time for the Messiah's appearance would be close at hand. He farther adds, that the rabbi in question flourished two hundred years after the birth of Christ. If this were the case, how can it be explained, that, knowing the predicted period had so long elapsed, he did not renounce the Mosaic law, and profess the Christian doctrine?

To vanquish these imaginary difficulties, represented by our author as so formidable, let the good father be informed, that the Jews will not deviate one iota from the literal meaning of the text, nor will they ever admit of converting the plain literal sense into allegory; but when any passage occurs which is obviously figurative, they will endeavor to resolve it into a sense as nearly approaching the literal as the text will allow.

Let him learn also, that the Talmud is composed of canons, dogmas, and regulations for the ritual; and that when in case of a doubt arising among the rabbins upon any point therein treated, after having been thoroughly discussed and canvassed in their *midrash,* or college, it has been solved and decided by a plurality of voices, conformably to the opinion that appears to carry with it the greatest weight: such decision is preserved and followed by the Jews, as rigidly as if it were the written law itself. On the other hand, as is well known, the Talmud contains an immense number of allegories in reference to every part of the Bible, which frequently give rise to questions that are agitated and investigated like the rest, but are never absolutely determined nor decided upon, and only serve to elicit some moral conclusions for the people, which, if well selected and well applied in sermons, are likely to produce useful effects on the congregation.

But to come more immediately to the point at issue, *i. e.* the closed or final *Mem* which occurs in the middle of the word, and which the Talmudists (if we may believe the preacher) understand to denote a number: I shall show, and with every appearance of probability, and in strict conformity with the circumstances of the times, that it may be accounted for by looking to the form of the letter itself.

God having promised the pious and devout King Hezekiah a solid and lasting peace, and a perpetual and uninterrupted tranquillity, not satisfied with having signified this in mere verbal language, placed in the middle of the word the final *Mem*, which being a close quadrangle, served the purpose of a hieroglyphic, to indicate to the king, that as this square is so shut in on all sides, that nothing can enter or break it, in like manner the peace he was to enjoy would not be interrupted or broken in upon during his whole life, as, in fact, turned out to be the case.

Here we perceive two allegories applied to this *Mem*, founded on two suppositions, both possible, both plausible, and both adequate. Let us examine the value and meaning of the Talmudic allegory, and how far it extends.

The Talmudic rabbi, according to the preacher, affirms, that the Messiah ought to come six hundred years after King Ahaz, in virtue of the closed or final *Mem:* well, so be it; but it is requisite to examine the qualification of this rabbi, and how he became enabled to fathom this recondite mystery, whether by reflection or by divine inspiration; if it were from the latter of these means, it becomes a sort of prophecy, and as such demands our implicit acquiescence; but if obtained from his own meditations and ideas, it is entitled to no greater influence or force than any other allegory; and being so, as, in fact, it is, there is no obligation to believe or receive it as if it were prophecy; on the contrary, the author himself only advances it as a mere conjecture, believing the event possible (at the time named), but not as sure to happen. This proves itself; for if the nation had received this prediction as prophetical, they would have acknowledged Christ to be the Messiah, that is to say, the Messiah promised in the closed *Mem*, but which they certainly did not.

LV.—It is ridiculous to object, as is done at the end of section fifty-three, that if the Jews deny that the *Mem* in *Lemarbè* signifies the six hundred years that elapsed between the fourth year of Ahaz and the coming of Christ, they would incur the penalty of death.

The Lord Archbishop is much mistaken; for the obligation on the Jews to believe the rabbins extends no farther than to the doctrine and the ritual of the Law, as we may perceive from chapter xvii. verses 8 to 14 of Deuteronomy. But they are not compelled to believe in every rabbinical allegory. I have already remarked, that if any rabbi makes an allegorical statement or exposition of any passage in the Holy Scriptures, which the preacher imagines may be turned to his own advantage, he presents it in argument to the Jews, as if it were with them an article of faith, and persuades himself that he has thereby brought conviction home to their minds. According to this doctrine, I, for my disbelief in the rabbinical exposition of the *Mem*, ought to be regarded by my nation as a heretic or schismatic; but this is far from being the case; for, as I have so often remarked, allegory is no more than a human idea, and as such not considered to carry with it any divine sanction; thus, the argument drawn from the numerical signification of the *Mem* falls to the ground, and needs no farther reply.

The author of this refutation, oppressed by age and infirmities, has had no opportunity to see the book quoted by the reverend preacher; but, having attentively examined the passage alluded to in the works of Maimonides himself, finds that the archbishop, with his accustomed candor, has given a garbled extract therefrom, omitting the commencement of the discourse, which is essential to the true understanding of the paragraph in question. The author writes as follows:*
"With regard to what you say relating to the period of the Messiah's coming, and what R. Saadya advances on the subject: first you ought to know that the precise time cannot be ascertained by any living being, as is declared in Daniel xii. 9, 'And he said, Go thy way, Daniel, for

---

* *Vide Epist. ad Orient.*

the words are closed up and sealed till the end of time.'

"However, ideas and opinions have been entertained by some learned men, who think they have ascertained it, and the prophet has touched on that point, saying, (Daniel xii. 4,) 'Though you extend and increase knowledge greatly,' &c., meaning, that although opinions would multiply and various judgments be formed concerning the Messiah's coming, still no human prediction of that event would be accomplished; the prophet goes on to admonish us, not on that account to doubt of the truth of God's promise, and says, 'Be not troubled if this be not accomplished at the time anticipated; but in proportion as his coming may be protracted, so let your hopes be increased;' as also says Habakkuk, chapter ii. verse 3, 'And though it tarries, wait for it, because it will surely come.'

"It deserves notice, that the period even of the Egyptian captivity, although to this God affixed a precise term (for we read in Genesis, chapter xv. verse 13, 'And they shall serve them, and be afflicted by them four hundred years,') is not exactly understood, being difficult to ascertain, some supposing that these four hundred years should be reckoned from the patriarch Jacob's going down into Egypt; others, from the time the captivity commenced, about seventy years later; others again were of opinion, that the period was to be reckoned from the time of the patriarch Abraham's receiving the revelation, and accordingly when the four hundred years of their reckoning were completed, certain Israelites left Egypt thirty years before the mission of Moses, thinking that the time of redemption had arrived; and they were slain by the Egyptians, who increased the yoke of the captivity: this at least we are taught by our sages; and David alludes to these men in Psalm lxxviii. verse 9, where he says, 'The children of Ephraim, armed and carrying bows, turned their back in the day of battle!'

"The true reckoning of the four hundred years was from the birth of Isaac, who was Abraham's successor, as we read in Genesis, chapter xxi. ver. 12, 'For in Isaac shall thy generation be called.' In Genesis, chapter xv. verse 13, God said, 'Your posterity shall be wanderers in a land not their own, and shall serve and be afflicted by them four hundred years.' The literal sense of this verse is, that during part of the captivity, the Egyptians would rule over them, humiliate, and afflict them, as there were to be, in all, four hundred years of exile, but not of subjection. This truth remained unknown, until it was found, after the coming of Moses, that the four hundred years were accomplished between the birth of Isaac and the departure from Egypt. We consequently may infer, that if the term of the Egyptian captivity, which had a fixed and limited period, was not rightly understood, how much less likely so to be is our present protracted captivity, which, from its extended duration, alarmed the prophets themselves, and prompted one of them to exclaim, Psalm lxxxiv. verse 5, 'Wilt thou be angry with us forever? Wilt thou extend thine anger to all generations?' And Isaiah, treating on the procrastination of the captivity, says, chapter xxiv. verse 22, 'And they shall be gathered together as prisoners are gathered in the dungeon, and shall be shut up in the prison, and after many days shall be visited.'"

From the above quotation, we perceive that the very learned author was of opinion, that no man can ever attain to a knowledge of the precise time of the Messiah's coming: in proof of which, he quotes the verse from Daniel, "That the prophecies will remain closed and sealed until the last hour;" and from this fact, he brings forward the example of the Egyptian captivity, to which, although God was pleased to affix a precise limit of four hundred years, there existed various suppositions and opinions concerning its duration, by reason of the uncertainty of the exact date from which the computation was to commence.

This eminent sage, after expressing himself so explicitly on this article, ventures to prescribe a period for the advent of the Messiah: knowing this fact, is there any person in the world (except the archbishop) who can fail to believe that this opinion is advanced, not as infallible, but merely as possible? If the preacher had been candid enough to produce the whole of the passage (as I have done), there would have been no foundation left for his arguments; but it was certain, that he had not to fear contradiction from those he was addressing, they being men condemned to the flames, suffering under penance, and wearing the badge of the Inquisition.

LVI.—In this number, our author adduces a sentence from one of the sages of the Talmud, who says that the world is to exist only six thousand years, "*Machini Mundi hujus annorum Sexies Milla, et non plurum persistere debet,*" and then adds, "the same say your rabbins, from ancient tradition since the time of Elijah's disciples."

The preacher here asserts two things:—First, that the rabbins affirm this from *ancient tradition*. Secondly, that this same tradition takes its origin from the disciples of Elijah, understanding this Elijah to be the prophet known by that name, who was taken up alive to heaven. But to prove how little the reverend father is versed in Hebrew literature, and how imperfect his acquaintance is with the Talmud, I will show that this is only the unsupported opinion of one of the sages, and not ancient tradition received from the time of Elijah's disciples; and in the course of the discussion it will appear who this Elijah actually was.

First, it is requisite to keep in mind, that in the Talmud, when a sage advances an opinion, whether originating in his own mind, or based on some passage in the Holy Scriptures, if it does not appertain to any part of the law, either ritual or doctrinal, it is not discussed nor decided, so that although sometimes the opinions of others are produced against it, the matter goes no farther.

The great Rabbi Moses of Egypt, in the last chapter of his commentary on Kings, treating on the different opinions in the Talmud, as to what is to happen before and after the coming of the Messiah, says, that these prophecies are very obscure and difficult to comprehend, that the prophets themselves did not understand them, that the sages did not receive any tradition concerning them, and that they only discoursed about them from what they collected from the text itself. Thus we find that this learned man, so eminent in the knowledge of the Talmud, asserts that the sages never received any tradition regarding these sayings and opinions, and that they formed their notions on them from conjecture; and this he follows up, by saying, that much time ought not to be bestowed on this study, since mere human conjectures often prove erroneous and rarely true!

Hence we perceive, that this opinion has never been received, either as an article of faith or tradition; and if the term of six thousand years had passed, we should be entitled to say, that it had not been justified by the event, or that it indicated, under a form of speech, something that we could not comprehend: and to show that it is not sanctioned by the Talmud, we find in the treatise *Sanhedrin*, chapter *Helek* (which he so frequently quotes), that a different opinion was entertained by another famous rabbi, who says that the reign of the Messiah in himself and in his descendants, is to last seven thousand years.

Our author farther affirms, that the doctrine of the six thousand years was an old tradition received by the Rabbins from the disciples of Elijah, and to give force to the argument, he leads us to understand that it was the prophet Elijah.

However, I beg to inform the Archbishop, that this same Elijah was only a rabbi, in whose house an academy was held; and when anything is recorded in his name, it is to be understood merely as having been discussed therein: and the same remark applies to Rabbi Ishmael, in whose house another academy was held, of which the proceedings are given in the same form; so this Elijah was just as much the prophet Elijah, as Rabbi Ishmael the son of the patriarch Abraham; consequently the tradition was not received from the disciples of Elijah, as the learned preacher has affirmed.

I cannot pass unnoticed the manner in which he has misrepresented the passage to which he refers; for in order to shape it to his taste, and to prevent the possibility of contradiction, he does not produce the text itself, but says the sages affirm that the world will exist only six thousand years,—the first two thousand under the Law of Nature, without the written law; the second two thousand, under the Law of Moses; and the last two thousand, under the Law of the Messiah.

But in fact, the sage expresses himself in the following manner:—"It was declared in the academy, or rather Elijah's house, that the world is to subsist six thousand years, and then for one thousand it is to remain waste; two thousand without any jurisdiction whatever; two thousand with the Law of Moses; and the last two thousand during the time of the Messiah."

We see then how the preacher perverts this opinion, and makes an addition, of his own invention, to the words of the sage, who merely says, that the last two thousand years will be those when the Messiah may or ought to come (that is to say, during any part of them, either at their beginning or end), but the preacher makes him declare that the last two thousand years are to be under the Law of the Messiah, indicative that the Law of Moses was then to cease, and that of Christ to be established; whereas the learned Elijah made no mention whatever of the *law* of the Messiah, but only of the *time* of the Messiah; his object being, by interpolating and corrupting the text, to represent the rabbins of the Talmud as believing in Christ. Men who argue in this manner expose themselves not only to the derision and scoff of the Jews, but also to the contempt of all well-informed Christians.

LVII.—The same reply may be made to his inference, drawn from the doctrine of the eighty-five jubilees, viz: that it is not received tradition, but merely individual opinion, and as such does not compel our belief. He adds that we ought to take counsel of a certain Rabbi Samuel, who, convinced by a similar train of reasoning, renounced our faith, and worshipped Christ; this same Rabbi Samuel having stated, that after turning over in his mind all that the prophets had said, he clearly understood that Christ was the son of God sent into the world for our redemption. I believe what he states, with regard to *turning over* the prophets; but I can assert, that *I* have studied them, and made them my principal occupation, during several years, but never found what this neophyte discovered; and I am confident that no one will make such a discovery, who carefully studies the prophecies, and not merely skims them over. Indeed the numerous proofs alleged by the archbishop go no farther, than to show the weakness of his arguments, and the slight foundation on which he builds his opinions.

He says that Rabbi Anima Voluntas, or Rabbi Moses of Egypt, for they are one and the same, also acknowledges this truth, as may be seen in *Sanhedrin, Gazit*, in the division *Helek;* for on the Jews inquiring of him the time of the Messiah's coming, this rabbi contemplating the procrastination of his and our hopes, in regard to the future advent of the Messiah answered them with this reproof, "*Vanum est atque inane a Judæis Messiam expectari, sed sola redemptio consistit in pœnitentiá.*"

I do not know who the Anima Voluntas, or Rabbi Moses the Egyptian, can be, who gave this opinion. Here is evidently an anachronism of seven or eight hundred years; for the Talmud was completed twelve or thirteen centuries back, whereas the only Rabbi Moses of Egypt I know, flourished but about six centuries ago.— What we do find in the chapter alluded to, is an expression of a very learned man, named Rab, who treating on the advent of the Messiah, says: "Already all the appointed periods of time are passed, and the event (namely the advent of the Messiah) now only depends on penitence and pious works."

He hereby intimates, that the present captivity has no prescribed term, as was the case with those of Egypt and Babylon (one of four hundred years, the other, of seventy), and that the periods supposed to have been set by Daniel, or others, having passed away, and the Messiah not yet come, the Jews ought now to undeceive themselves, and learn that the coming of the Messiah rests only on penitence and good works, and does not depend on any fixed epoch. It seems to me impossible to collect from these words of the sage, that he understood that the Messiah had already come.

LVIII.—LXIII.—In these sections, our author gives an elaborate history of various pseudo-Messiahs, that have appeared in the nation during a period of more than fifteen hundred years. To all this it may be answered, that although it be true the people ran to receive some of them, flattering themselves with the belief that each might be the true and expected Messiah, so soon as they saw that the prophecies which regard the true Messiah were not literally fulfilled in them, they rejected and abandoned them, looking upon them in the light in which they are still held by the nation, as mere impostors.

Is it any wonder that an abject and oppressed people should seize every opportunity to effect their deliverance, being led away by that confidence which they always had, and still have, in God, and by the hope they place in His divine and holy word, which cannot fail?

Did there not exist, and do there not exist at

the present day in Portugal, persons who expect the return of King Sebastian;* and was there not, in past ages, one who pretended to be the same, and were not books written to prove him such? If, then, such things have occurred in a free nation, merely from the anxious wish of beholding again a beloved monarch, can it be surprising that an oppressed people, actuated by the fond hope of seeing a king promised to them by the Almighty, should fall into a similar error?

LXIV.—In this section, our author questions the Jews seriously, if they expect the Messiah to come with those signs that the Scriptures and the prophets describe, or with others, of which no mention is made?

I reply to the archbishop, that the Messiah we expect is the same that is described in the Holy Scriptures; and if he wishes to know for what purpose he is to come, and what he will effect, let him read the following prophecies:

Deuteronomy xxx. 1-10. "And it shall come to pass, when all these things are come upon thee, the blessing and the curse, which I have set before thee, and thou shalt call them to mind

---

*King Don Sebastian was supposed, in former ages, to have mysteriously disappeared from Portugal, and numbers of his subjects verily believed he would return to them at some future period; and there used to be, in Lisbon, one particular road by which many imagined he would come.

among all the nations whither the Lord thy God hath driven thee, and shalt return unto the Lord thy God, and shalt obey his voice according to all that I command thee this day, thou and thy children, with all thine heart, and all thy soul: that then the Lord thy God will turn thy captivity, and have compassion upon thee, and will return and gather thee from all the nations, whither the Lord thy God hath scattered thee. If any of thine be driven out into the uttermost parts of heaven, from there will the Lord thy God gather thee, and from there will he fetch thee; and the Lord thy God will bring thee into the land which thy fathers possessed, and thou shalt possess it; and he will do thee good, and multiply thee above thy fathers; and the Lord thy God will circumcise thine heart, and the heart of thy seed, to love the Lord thy God with all thine heart, and with all thy soul, that thou mayest live; and the Lord thy God will put all these curses upon thine enemies, and on them that hate thee, who have persecuted thee; and thou shalt return and obey the voice of the Lord, and do all his commandments, which I command thee this day; and the Lord thy God will make thee plenteous in every work of thine hand, in the fruit of thy body, and in the fruit of thy cattle, and in the fruit of thy land for good; for the Lord will again rejoice over thee for good, as he rejoiced over thy fathers; if thou wilt hearken unto the voice of the Lord thy God, to keep his commandments, and his statutes, which are written in the book of the law, and if thou turn unto the Lord thy God with all thine heart and with all thy soul."

From these verses it must be inferred, that even after the advent of the Messiah, the law of Moses will be observed by His people.

Isaiah, chapter ii. verses 2–4. "And it shall come to pass in the last days, that the mountain of the Lord's house shall be established on the top of the mountains, and shall be exalted above the hills, and all nations shall flow unto it. And many people shall go and say, Come ye, and let us go up to the mountain of the Lord, to the house of the God of Jacob; and he will teach us of his ways, and we will walk in his paths; for out of Zion shall go forth the law, and the word of the Lord from Jerusalem. And he shall judge among the nations, and shall rebuke many people, and they shall beat their swords into ploughshares, and their spears into pruning-hooks; nation shall not lift up sword against nation, neither shall they learn war any more."

Ibid., chapter xi. verses 10–16. "And in that day there shall be a root of Jesse, which shall stand for an ensign of the people, to it shall the gentiles seek, and his rest shall be glorious. And it shall come to pass in that day, that the Lord shall set his hand again the second time to recover the remnant of his people, which shall be left from Assyria, and from Egypt, and from Pathros, and from Cush, and from Elam, and from Shinar, and from Hamath, and from the islands of the sea. *And he shall set up an ensign for the nations, and shall assemble the outcasts of Israel, and gather together the dispersed of Judah from the four corners of the earth.* The envy also of Ephraim shall depart, and the adversaries of Judah shall be cut off: Ephraim shall not envy Judah, and Judah shall not vex Ephraim. But they shall fly upon the shoulders of the Philistines towards the West; they shall spoil them of the East together; they shall lay their hand upon Edom and Moab, and the children of Ammon shall obey them. And the Lord shall utterly destroy the tongue of the Egyptian sea, and shall wave his hand over the river, and with his mighty winds shall smite it into seven streams, and make men go over dry-shod! And there shall be a highway for the remnant of his people, which shall be left from Assyria, like as it was to Israel in the day that he came up out of the land of Egypt."

Ibid., lii. 1. "Awake, awake: put on thy strength, O Zion; put on thy beautiful garments, O Jerusalem, the holy city! for henceforth there shall no more come into thee the uncircumcised and the unclean."

Ibid., chapter lxv. verses 16, 19, and 20. "He who blesseth himself on the earth shall bless himself in the God of Truth, and he that sweareth on the earth shall swear by the God of Truth; because the former troubles are forgotten, and because they are hid from mine eyes! . . . . I will rejoice in Jerusalem, and joy in my people, and the voice of weeping shall no more be heard in her, nor the voice of crying. There shall be no more thence an infant of days, nor an old man that hath not filled his days; for the child shall die a hundred years old; but the sinner being a hundred years old shall be accursed." And so throughout the chapter.

Ibid., chapter lxvi. 18, 19, and 20. "For I know their works and their thoughts; it shall come that I will gather all nations and tongues, and they shall see my glory. And I will set among them a sign, and I will send those that escape of them unto the nations Tarshish, Pul, and Lud, that draw the bow, to Tubal and Javan, to the isles afar off, that have not heard my fame, neither have seen my glory, and they shall declare my glory among the gentiles. And they shall bring all your brethren for an offering unto the Lord out of all nations, upon horses and in chariots, and in litters, and upon mules, and upon swift beasts, to my holy mountain, Jerusalem, saith the Lord, as the children of Israel bring an offering in a clean vessel into the house of the Lord."

Jeremiah, chapter iii. verses 17 and 18. "At that time they shall call Jerusalem the throne of the Lord, and all the nations shall be gathered into it to the name of the Lord to Jerusalem, neither shall they walk any more after the imagination of their evil hearts. In those days the house of Judah shall walk with the house of Israel, and they shall come together out of the land of the north, to the land which I have given for an inheritance to your fathers."

Ibid., chapter xxxi. verse 34. "And they shall no more teach every man his neighbor and every man his brother, saying, Know the Lord; for they shall all know me, from the least of them even unto the greatest of them, saith the Lord; for I will forgive their iniquity, and I will remember their sin no more."

Ezekiel, chap. xxxvi. verses 25 and 26. "Then I will sprinkle clean water upon you, and ye shall be clean, from all your filthiness, and from all your idols will I cleanse you. A new heart also will I give you, and a new spirit will I put within you, and I will take away the stony heart out of your flesh, and I will give you a heart of flesh."

Ibid., chapter xxxvii. verses 24–28. " And David my servant shall be king over them; and they shall have one shepherd; they shall also walk in my judgments, and observe my statutes and do them. And they shall dwell in the land that I have given unto Jacob my servant, wherein your fathers have dwelt, and they shall dwell therein, even they and their children, and their children's children for ever, and my servant David shall be their prince forever. Moreover I will make a covenant of peace with them; it shall be an everlasting covenant with them, and I will place them and multiply them, and will set my sanctuary in the midst of them forevermore. My tabernacle also shall be with them: yea, I will be their God, and they shall be my people. And the heathen shall know that I the Lord do sanctify Israel, when my sanctuary shall be in the midst of them forevermore."

Ibid., chapter xxxix. verses 27–29. "When I have brought them again from the people, and gathered them out of their enemies' lands, and am sanctified in them in the sight of many nations; then shall they know that I am the Lord their God, who caused them to be led into captivity among the heathen, but I have gathered them into their own, and have left none of them any more there. Neither will I hide my face any more from them; for I have poured out my Spirit upon the house of Israel, saith the Lord God."

Joel, chapter ii. verses 27–29. "And ye shall know that I am in the midst of Israel, and that I am the Lord your God, and none else, and my people shall never be ashamed. And it shall come to pass afterwards, that I will pour out my spirit upon all flesh, and your sons and your daughters shall prophesy, your old men shall dream dreams, and your young men shall see visions. And also upon all the servants and the handmaids in those days will I pour out my spirit."

Ibid., chapter iii. verses 16, 17. "And the Lord also shall roar out of Zion, and utter his voice from Jerusalem, and the heavens and the earth shall shake; but the Lord will be the hope of his people, and the strength of the children of Israel. So shall ye know that I am the Lord your God, dwelling in Zion, my holy mountain: then shall Jerusalem be holy, and there shall no strangers pass through her any more."

Zechariah, chapter viii. verse 23. "Thus saith the Lord of Hosts, In those days it shall come to pass, that ten men shall take hold, out of all languages of the nations, even shall take hold of the skirt of him that is a Jew, saying, We will go with you; for we have heard that God is with you."

Ibid., chapter xiv. verse 16. "And it shall come to pass, that every one that is left of all the nations which came up against Jerusalem, shall even go up from year to year to worship the King, the Lord of Hosts, and to keep the feast of tabernacles."

Daniel, chap. ii. ver. 44: "And in the days of these kings shall the God of heaven set up a kingdom, which shall never be destroyed, and the kingdom shall not be left to other people; but it shall break in pieces, and consume all these kingdoms, and it shall stand forever."

Such is the indelible character of the Messiah and the touchstone by which the truth of his mission must be tested; for if in his time all these prophecies are accomplished (and an infinite number of others which I omit), we shall acknowledge him as such; but if not, we shall regard him as spurious, and we shall not judge figuratively, but literally; for if we take the liberty to turn the prophecies, which stand in no need of a figurative construction, into allegories, how would it be possible to distinguish the false from the true Messiah?

Whoever might be disposed to apply them to himself by perverting the text, and allegorizing it to suit his purpose, might set himself up for the Messiah, whereas the realization of the undermentioned chain of events, forms an unerring criterion by which the true Messiah can be ascertained: he must be known and made manifest in the eyes of all the nations of the earth; in his time war is to cease among the nations; all will follow one only law; and adore one only God.—Now, as we have not to this day seen any of these prophecies accomplished, we must conclude that the Messiah has not yet come.

LXIV.—In this section our author quotes the eighth chapter, fourteenth verse of Isaiah, allegorizing it as usual. It has already been proved, that this chapter, the preceding and subsequent ones, treat of King Hezekiah, and no more need be added on this point.

LXV.—LXIX.—In this he pretends to prove, that verses 3, 4, and 5 of chapter iii. of Hosea, treat of Christ, and then proceeds to say, the prophet Hosea, (chap. iii.,) gave us another sign from which the Messiah may be recognised; "*Dies multos expectabis me et ego expectabo vos.*"— "When the Messiah is come," says the prophet, "the Jews will be still waiting for him, and the Messiah will wait for the Jews; and because the Jews will not receive him, they will continue without a king, without a prince, without sacrifice, and without an altar." "*Sedebunt filii Israel sine rege, sine principe, sine sacrificio, et sine altari.*" After the Jews have remained in this state, they will acknowledge the Messiah whom they would not receive when he did come, "*et post hæc revertentur filii Israel ad Dominum Deum suum et ad David regum suum.*"

For the better comprehending of this prophecy, and to convince the world how little reason the reverend preacher evinces in his remarks upon it, it will be requisite to give the quotation from beginning to end.

Hosea, iii. 1-5.—"*Et dixit Dominus ad me, Adhuc vade, dilige mulierem dilectam socii et adulteram, secundum dilectionem Domini ad filios Israel, et ipsi respicientes ad Deos alienos et diligentes dolia uvarum; et mercatus sum eam mihi, in quindecim argenteis et chomer hordeorum et letech hordeorum, et dixi ad eam, Dies multos sedebis mihi; ne fornicaberis, et ne sis viro, et etiam ego ad te. Quia dies multos manebunt filii Israel, non rex et non princeps, et non sacrificium, et non statua, et non ephod et teraphim. Postea revertentur filii Israel et quærent Dominum Deum suum, et David regem suum, et pavebunt ad Dominium et ad bonum ejus in novissimo dierum."*

"Then said the Lord unto me, Go, yet love a woman (beloved of her friend, yet, an adulteress), according to the love of the Lord towards the children of Israel, who look to other gods, and love flagons of wine. So I bought her to me, for fifteen pieces of silver, and for an homer of barley, and a half homer of barley. And I said unto her, Thou shalt abide for me many days, thou shalt not play the harlot, and thou shalt not be for another man: so will I also be for thee. For the children of Israel shall abide many days without a king, without a prince, and without a sacrifice, and without an image, and without ephod or teraphim. Afterward shall the children of Israel return penitently and seek the Lord their God and David their king, and shall fear the Lord and his goodness in the latter days."

God told the prophet to take a woman, and love her as a faithful husband, notwithstanding her being an adulteress.

The prophecy declares thus much, and its interpretation exactly corresponds. God loved and favored Israel, notwithstanding their being plunged into the idolatry of the Egyptians, He gave the law which was the espousal; but they were ungrateful, and gave themselves up to idolatry and vice, and particularly to wine.

The prophet says, that he took his wife for fifteen pieces of silver and an homer and a half of barley, and made a compact with her that she should continue many days without knowing any other man, or even himself.

He gives the allegory, and then applies it by saying:—For in the same manner that this woman would remain without a husband, and without a lover, for penalty of her past adulteries, the children of Israel would remain many days without a king (of the house of David), without a prince (of the kings of Israel), without sacrifice (that is without the temple), without a statue (that is without idolatry), without ephod, namely, without Urim and Thummim (which constituted the divine oracle), through which the prince consulted God, and without teraphim (that is, the oracle of the heathen).

Thus the type exactly corresponds with the event; for in like manner as the prophet's wife was to pass many days without a husband, and at the same time free from adultery, so Israel in her captivity was to remain without sacrifice, without a temple (indicating the husband), without an image, meaning idolatry, (which is adultery,) without the ephod (which is prophecy), and even without the oracles of the gentiles from which to learn future events.

The prophet farther says, that when the period was past, in which the people of Israel should have given proofs of their great constancy, and their confidence in God, they would return to repentance for the sins they had committed, and would thus obtain the manifest interposition of divine providence in their favor, by the restoration of their temple, and the reign of the house of David, all which should come to pass in the latter days.

This is the literal sense of the prophecy.

Not content with explaining away its sense in metaphors, the reverend preacher boldly alters the words of the text, wishing us to believe that God said, "*Dies multos expectabis me, et ego expectabo vos.*" And on this falsified text remarks, "When the Messiah comes, the Jews will still wait for him, and the Messiah will have to wait for the Jews; and because the Jews will not receive him, they will remain without a king," &c.

From what part of the prophecy, is it to be deduced that the Jews would reject the Messiah? and that because the Jews would not receive him, they were to remain without a king, &c.? Is not the punishment of being without a king the penalty for having committed adultery, that is to say, idolatry?

What the prophet says is diametrically opposite to what the preacher has pretended to infer; for Hosea affirms, that they shall be many days without a king, prince, or sacrifice, and that afterwards they will return in penitence and seek God, and David their king. But the preacher asserts, that they are to remain without a king, &c., after the coming of the Messiah, in consequence of not having acknowledged him; now from which of the words of the prophet does he infer that on the Messiah's coming, he was to be rejected by the Jews, and that the Messiah was to be both God and Man? In order to show clearly the true source from which the preacher draws these two conclusions, we must place in a clear light, the corruptions that he has introduced into the text, on the strength of which he expects to make his assertions pass current with the Jews. We will produce his alleged quotations from the prophet, and compare with the original.

Preacher.	Original.
Dies multos expectabis me, et ego expectabo vos.	*Et dixit ad eam, Dies multos sedebis mihi, ne fornicaberis, et ne sis viro, et etiam ego ad te.*
Post hæc revertentur filii Israel ad Dominum Deum suum, et ad David regem suum.	*Postea revertentur filii Israel et querent Dominum Deum suum, et David regem suum.*

Wishing to make the prophet appear to say,

that the Jews had to wait for the Messiah, and the Messiah for the Jews, he interpolates a verse, for which there is no authority in the sacred text, "*Dies multos expectabis me, et ego expectabo vos;*" "many days you will expect me, and I shall have to expect you," as if thereby intimating that he came, but was not received by the Jews, for whom he is still patiently waiting.

Now in the first place, this verse has been forged either by the Lord Archbishop, or by the authors of the vulgate; for there is no such sentence to be found in the prophecy. Secondly, did there even exist such a verse, it would not allude to the Messiah, but to the prophet himself, since the former is not introduced as speaking in any part of the prophecy; consequently, not even by corrupting the text, as he has done, does our author advance his argument a single step. The prophecy cannot be understood to apply to Christ in any manner; for it states that after the children of Israel have been for many days without a king, prince, or sacrifice, they will become penitent and seek God and the Messiah. Ergo—after Israel remaining a long time without a king, &c., the Messiah was to come. But when Christ came, Israel did not lack a king, temple, or sacrifice; so that Christ could not be the Messiah promised in the prophecy.

I will now turn to the corruption in the other

verse "*Et postea revertentur filii Israel ad Dominum Deum suum, et ad David regem suum.*" Now the original says, "*Postea revertentur filii Israel et querent Dominum Deum suum, et David regem suum.*" The omission of the word *querent*, makes the text read as if the children of Israel would return penitent to God, and to David their king; by which the author imagines that he has gained his point of showing that the Messiah is to be God and man. However, he will find that if he can bring no better proofs in support of his doctrine than these, they will not avail him much; since in the original Hebrew, and in every Bible, whether in print, or in manuscript, we find ובקשו, which means *et querent*, and is so translated in all the various versions which exist in different languages and is similarly rendered by Pagnino, Arius Montanias, and many others.

Jonathan the son of Uziel, in the Targum, writes, that they will return penitent; that they will seek their God, and obey the Messiah, the son of David; consequently he does not hold him to be God. How wretched must be the reasoning derived from such fabrications! That he should preach them I am not surprised, there being no one present who knew how, or could venture to contradict him; but I do wonder that any one should have the audacity to send them to the public press, regardless of the disgrace brought upon those who appear to countenance such corruptions of the Divine word. It is, indeed, grievous and lamentable that men should be found so blind as to introduce corruptions into the sacred text, and persist in them, for their selfish purposes, which amounts to an act of treason against the Divine Majesty; which cannot please even those persons of their own faith, whose understandings are free to discuss truth, and who must detest the use of such means: much less will they convince the Jews, who are the depositaries of the Divine word, and the ark, wherein the testimony is preserved pure, clear, and immaculate, from which the learned, even of the Christian religion, form their translations, and which they adopt as their guide, and appeal to in all cases of doubt.

LXX.—The preacher produces the prophecy of Malachi, chap. i. ver. 10 and 11. "I have no pleasure in you, saith the Lord of Hosts, neither will I accept an offering at your hand; for from the rising of the sun even unto the going down of the same, my name is great among the gentiles, and in every place incense is offered to my name, and a pure offering; for my name is great among the heathen, saith the Lord of Hosts."

The reverend preacher supposes that the prophet speaks of the time of Christ, and thence deduces that God had destroyed the nation, and the sacrifices, and pretends to prove that He had created a new and pure sacrifice in its stead, one who sacrificed himself for the whole world, and by whose means the name of God has become great throughout the globe; and that the prophet alludes to him when he says, "For from the rising of the sun to the going down thereof, my name is great among the gentiles, and in every place incense and pure gifts are offered to my name."

His great argument against the Jews, and on which he founds his exposition, consists in this, that at the time of the prophet there was no nation that offered sacrifice to God; and therefore, of necessity, he must be speaking of the time of Christ, to whose name, throughout the four quarters of the globe, a pure sacrifice was offered.

To reply to this would-be formidable argument, it is proper to remark that Malachi was the last of all the prophets, and entered upon his mission in the early days of the Second Temple, when the priesthood were grossly ignorant of their duties, as we perceive from the prophet Haggai, his contemporary, chapter ii. verses 12 and 13; for, on his asking them a question relative to their office, their ignorance was made manifest by the nature of their reply; nor is it to be wondered at that having been seventy years out of the ministry, they had forgotten the theory as well as the practice. In addition to their general state of ignorance, the people became infected by the example of the surrounding nations, and, like them, were wanting in the true feeling of devotion; and when they offered sacrifice to God, they sought for some animal which was lame or blind, or which they had stolen, to avoid giving of their own; and set so little value upon their burnt offerings and sacrifices, that they thought the worst subjects they could find were good enough for the altar. This occurred among the lower orders. The priests, who, as being nearest to God, we might have expected would reprove the people, and clearly show them their errors, were the very persons who encouraged and promoted this sin, by speaking irreverently of the holy altar, complaining of their labor, and neglecting their sacred duties. By this reprehensible conduct they destroyed all devotion among the people, and incurred the divine wrath; so that, being greatly incensed at the neglect and improper conduct of the priests, God sent to correct them through his holy prophet, recapitulating the loving kindness He had shown to the nation from the time of its origin in the patriarch Jacob.— Thus, this prophecy commences by setting before them the love which He had promised them, as contrasted with the fate of Esau, Jacob's own brother, whom God had deprived of his condition and kingdom, and converted his verdant and fertile land into a fearful desert, which was to continue waste forever,—so that he would never succeed, whatever exertions he might make to re-establish himself and rebuild his ruined cities; for all that he might build God would pull down, because his wickedness and sins had made him the object of divine wrath, and that, as such, he should be known and called among the nations; but that, on the other hand, He would establish *Israel*, and restore him to his original condition.

After enumerating the favors which He had bestowed on them, and continued to bestow, He goes on to relate the ingratitude with which they repaid these benefits, both people and priests; the former in bringing what was most vile and despicable for their sacrifices; the latter by offering such sacrifices and neglecting the divine ministry, for which reason He says, "I have no pleasure in you, nor are your offerings acceptable from your hands." Upon this the preacher puts the question, what sacrifice it was which the nations sacrificed in the time of the prophets, that was acceptable to God, as pure and clean, and who it was that caused the name of God to be promulgated and proclaimed throughout the world, from where the sun rises to where it sets, since God himself has declared that His name was great among the nations: from this inquiry our author concludes, that the circumstances could not have referred to the prophet's own time, for at that period the gentiles had no knowledge of a First Cause, and that consequently he must allude to the time of Christ.

It would be easy to answer the preacher, and overturn his objections, by the authority of the Targum of Jonathan, the son of Uziel, who explains these gifts and pure offerings to mean the prayers of the Jews in all countries.

Jonathan writes thus: "From the place were the sun rises unto the place where it sets, great is my name among the nations, and at all times that you shall perform my will, I will receive your prayers, and my great name shall be sanctified by your means, and your prayers shall be as pure sacrifice before me."

Thus this sage understands that the sacrifices alluded to, mean the orisons of the Jews, and these he calls pure sacrifice, and (in the opinion of this author) the Jews are the persons who sanctify the great name of God among the nations. Resting upon his sanction, I might claim the victory over my antagonist, were I as little scrupulous as himself; but, although Jonathan is a writer of no mean authority, and deservedly held in high estimation, *that* is not sufficient to oblige us to admit his allegory, and make us abandon the literal sense of the text; therefore, I contend, in opposition to his opinion, that the prophecy refers literally to the gentiles, and not to the Jews; this is in accordance with the views of the majority of the commentators upon the passage, who understood the prophet to mean, that the Divine Majesty reproaches the Jewish people and their priests for the contempt they evince in the sacrifices; adding, that He esteems the offering of the gentiles more than the oblations of the Jews; for, although the former were idolators, they had a knowledge of and adored a First Cause, as existing prior to all things, and Him they held to be from all eternity, although at the same time they admitted the existence of secondary causes. These gentiles, when they brought their sacrifices, notwithstanding they were offered up to idols, took peculiar care that they should be of the most perfect and pure kind that could be procured, while the Jews, although sacrificing to the true God, brought the worst they could find; for which reason God says, that the sacrifice of the gentiles was more pure than that of the Jews.

Let us examine into the true spirit of the prophecy, and we shall see how the good archbishop corrupts and perverts its meaning, to make it indicate the contrary of what it actually expresses. The prophecy consists in rebuking and reprimanding the people for the little respect with which they treated the sacrifices, reproaching them, that those which the gentiles (although idolators) presented were pure and immaculate, but that *they* selected the most worthless for their offerings; and concludes, in chapter iii., that after the advent of the Messiah, the offerings of Judah and Jerusalem would be acceptable to God, as in former days and in years of old.

The preacher, to evade any discussion concerning the mode in which the gentiles offered sacrifices to God at that time, boldly affirms, that the prophet treats of times subsequent to the advent of the Messiah, whom, because the Jews would not receive as the true Messiah, they and their sacrifices would be no longer acceptable to God; but, in lieu thereof, He would accept the sacrifice of the mass, which he calls pure and immaculate, offered up from the place where the sun rises unto where it sets, by the converted gentiles. He bases his exposition on a few isolated passages, irrespective of their connection with the context, which he takes care to suppress in all such places as would militate against his own views of the prophecy. But how can he attempt to argue that circumstances, which were to occur four or five hundred years later, could serve as an example or comparison to the Jews of that day? The prophet says, at that time the name of God was great and renowned among the nations, and that the gentiles then sacrificed to the Eternal Cause, and burnt incense, and presented to Him a pure offering: now, the preacher will not admit of this, until five hundred years afterwards. It must be noticed that he does not say, that the gifts and offerings of the gentiles were pleasing to God, but merely that their sacrifices were pure; not that God accepted and valued them, but only that they were consecrated to God; and affirms, that after the advent of the Messiah, the offerings of Judah and Jerusalem will be again acceptable to God; consequently, that God would not destroy the Jews, nor reject their offerings, but, on the contrary, would esteem and be pleased with them subsequent to the advent of the Messiah. The offerings of the gentiles never were grateful to Him, nor did He value them, and the comparison was only instituted to depreciate the sacrifices that the Jews brought in those days, and not to exalt those of others. I have been induced to present the whole of the prophecy, and to explain it, in order to show clearly, to all those who wish to learn the truth, the devices and corruptions that the preacher has made use of to maintain his hypothesis, and to let the impartial reader see how little cause he has to triumph on the scale of prophecy, which he twists and corrupts, so as to make it express what is convenient to himself, as "if there were no sons in Israel, as if he had no heir."

It remains to be shown, that in those times the gentiles had a knowledge of the First Cause, and that, although they recognised secondary causes, they nevertheless made a wide distinction between these and the First and Eternal

One; and although it may not be necessary to confirm what God himself declares (for independent of all human tradition, that would be sufficient in itself to settle the question), still it may be well to adduce some few authorities from Christian and gentile writers on the subject, which, while they deprive the preacher's argument of all its force, will make the meaning of the prophecy appear additionally clear and intelligible. I will not embarrass my answer with a multitude of quotations, but confine myself to such as come nearest to the point in question, since my chief object is confined to showing my own people what little cause the preacher has to assume to himself the victory, from passages bearing a sense so opposite to what he attempts to deduce from them; I will, therefore, content myself with citing only those which are most appropriate, and coincide nearly with the period in which the prophet lived: any one wishing to ascertain the truth may consult the originals.

Eusebius, in his work, "De Preparatione Evangelii," says he had read in a book of Zoroaster, the ancient Persian philosopher, the following words: "God is the first of all incorruptible beings, everlasting and inconceivable. He is not composed of parts. There is none comparable or equal to Him. He is the author of all good, totally independent, and the most exalted of the most excellent beings, the wisest of all intellects, the father of equity, and propagator of all good laws, omniscient, omnipotent, and the original Framer of nature."

Plutarch, in his treatise of Isis and Osiris, assures us that the Magi called *Oramazes* the great God, or the principle of light that produced all things, and operates all in all. They admitted of another god, but of an inferior nature, whom they called Mithras, or the inferior god, but did not consider him co-eternal with the supreme God, but the first product of his power.

Plutarch also, in the same treatise, speaking of the Egyptians, assures us, "that they held the opinion, that as the sun was common to all the world, although bearing different names in divers regions, so there exists only one Supreme intelligence and reason, one same Providence who governs the world, although worshipped under various names, and that He has deputed inferior beings to be His ministers."

Jamblicus says, according to the Egyptians, the Supreme Chief God existed in isolated unity prior to all other existences.

The author of the "Argonautica," says: "Let us first chaunt a hymn on ancient chaos; as the heavens, the seas, and the earth were formed out of it. Let us sing praises to that eternal, wise, and perfect Love that reduced this chaos into order."

Thales, the Milesian, one of the seven wise men

of Greece, who flourished about six hundred years before Christ (according to Diog. Laert., book I.), believed "that God is the most ancient of all beings, the author of the universe which is replete with wonders, the mind that redeemed it from confusion and reduced it into order, that He has no beginning nor end, and that nothing is hidden from Him, that there are none who can resist the force of destiny; but that this destiny is nothing more than the immutable reason and eternal power of Providence."

Pythagoras gives us an idea of the divinity in the following words: "There is but one only God, who is not, as some imagine, seated on the summit of the world, and on the circumference of the universe, but is in himself all in all; He sees all the existences which pervade infinite space; He is the sole first cause, the light of heaven, the father of all; He creates all things, orders and disposes of all; He is the reason, the life, and motion of all existences."

Plato, in his "Republica," says that "God is surrounded by a thick darkness which no mortal can penetrate, and that, as an inaccessible Deity, He ought to be adored in silence."

For farther proof of this truth, and to render it irrefutable, read in Daniel the idea which Nebuchadnezzar entertained of *one only God;* for immediately on Daniel's relating to him the dream of the statue, he acknowledged that his

God was the supreme God of gods; he does not say that he gained from this dream the knowledge of there being one God above all gods, but affirms that, by the miracle, he was made to know that the God whom Daniel adored was the true God of all gods.

Cyrus says, Ezra, chapter i. verses 2, 3, "The Lord God of heaven has bestowed on me all the kingdoms of the earth, and has commanded me to erect a temple in Jerusalem, which is in Judea; whoever desireth to be among you, and others of his own people, God be with him; let him go up to Jerusalem and build the house of the Lord God of Israel: *He is the God.*"

The Gibeonites deceived the princes of the nation, in the time of Joshua, with a well known stratagem, saying, that they had come from a far country, occupying six months' journey, on learning the name and fame of the miracles of the true God; and although it was but a fraud, it necessarily must have appeared credible at the time, that those remote nations had obtained a knowledge of the greatness of a First Cause; for were this not the case, the princes would not have been deceived, nor would the Gibeonites have dared to practise a deception based upon an impossibility.

God affirms that the wonders and signs he had wrought in Egypt, were only for the purpose of making known his name and fame throughout the world, "That my name may be declared throughout the earth." (Exod. chapter ix. verse 6.) It is clear, therefore, that the One First Cause was publicly acknowledged among all nations and worshipped, although under different names. It is not strange that this knowledge should have existed among them; for Nebuchadnezzar had proclaimed at divers times throughout his vast empire, that there was but the one God of the heavens, as seen in Daniel, chapter iv. verse 1, "Nebuchadnezzar, the king, to all people, nations, and languages that inhabit the earth. May peace be multiplied unto you. I deem it right to show the signs and wonders that the High God hath wrought towards me. How great are His signs and how powerful His miracles! His kingdom is an everlasting kingdom, and His dominion will endure from generation to generation." And in chapter iv. verse 37, varying the expression, he says, "Now I, Nebuchadnezzar, praise, extol, and glorify the King of heaven; for all His works are truth, and His ways justice, and those who walk in arrogance He is able to abase."

When Daniel was delivered from the lions, King Darius, the Mede, ordered the publishing of an edict, as follows, Daniel, chapter vi. verse 25–28: "Then King Darius wrote to all people, nations, and tongues, inhabiting all the earth, May peace be multiplied unto you. I make a decree, that in every region of my kingdom men tremble and fear before the God of Daniel; for he is the living God and established forever, and His kingdom shall not be destroyed, and His dominion shall be unto the end: He delivereth, and rescueth, and worketh signs and wonders in heaven and earth, who hath delivered Daniel from the power of the lions."

Cyrus, the king, ordered that there should be given to the holy temple, sheep, goats, lambs, salt, and wine, and oil, that they might sacrifice for the life of the king and the royal household; the edict is as follows, Ezra, chapter vi. verse 9, 10: "And whatever might be required, goats, sheep, or lambs, for a burnt offering to the God of heaven, also flour, salt, and oil, conformable to what the priests who are in Jerusalem may ask, shall be given daily without any hindrance, in order that they may offer a sweet savor to the God of heaven, and pray for the life of the king and his sons."

The King Artaxerxes sent considerable presents, and all other requisites, to the temple of God, as we see in Ezra, chapter vii. verses 21–23. "And I, King Artaxerxes, do command all treasurers who dwell on the other side of the river, that whatever Ezra, the priest, the scribe of the Law of God, may require, shall be given unto him. All things commanded by the God of heaven, shall be promptly done for the house of the

God of the heavens, that His anger may not be against the king's dominions or sons."

From all these instances, we may infer that the great name of God, and the knowledge of the First Cause, had been proclaimed and disseminated among the nations, and was revered and esteemed from the place where "the sun rises unto where he sets;" for the signs and miracles which God had wrought by the hands of His prophets and servants, had been made public by the three kings, Nebuchadnezzar, Darius, and Cyrus; and the Prophet Malachi living very near those times (at the commencement of the second temple), it is no wonder that a knowledge of the First Cause should have existed in the world in his days, and that the gentiles who had learned the truth should offer up to Him incense and sacrifice.

To these the prophet refers, when he says,— "That in all places they bring incense and pure offerings to my name."

It having now been proved, from both sacred and profane history, that the gentiles contemporary with the prophet Malachi had a full knowledge of the First Cause, and that many of them offered up sacrifices to Him and brought contributions: the prophecy becomes perfectly intelligible when taken with reference to the time of its promulgation; nor is there any necessity to torture it, as the preacher has done, in order to draw inferences contrary to its obvious and genuine sense.

The preacher, exhorting one of the prisoners who was brought out to be consigned to the flames, addresses him in these words: "Consider yourself in the presence of God, free from any other sin but that of reverencing the law of Moses; and imagine a Christian in the same presence, without any other crime than the observance of the law of Christ. If God condemned the Christian for his love of the law, and saved the Jew for his love of the same, God would not be just, nor could any satisfactory reply be given to the reasons the Catholic might in that case allege against His justice. For, under these circumstances, the Catholic would reason with God in the following manner:

"'Upright Judge, I believe in Christ, because he possessed all such signs as were revealed through thy prophets, that thy son should bring with him. I have done what Thou commandedst me; Thou hast condemned me for so doing; how canst Thou blame me for having obeyed thy commands?' These arguments are certainly unanswerable; consequently it is impossible that God should condemn a Catholic for being a Christian."

The archbishop speaks with as much effrontery as if he were secretary to the Supreme Being, and as if what passes in heaven were familiarly known to him; and has sufficient assurance and presumption to affirm that if God condemned the Catholic for observing the law of Christ, and saved the Jew for observing the law of Moses, God would not be just; and goes as far as to assert, that God could not reply satisfactorily to the arguments the Catholic might allege against His justice. The only reason adduced for the Catholic's believing in Christ is, because he contained in himself all the signs that God had revealed through His prophets that were to accompany His son.

But, should God reply to this Catholic that the Divine Majesty never had a son, and that in Christ those prophecies which relate to the true Messiah were not literally fulfilled; that none lead to considering the Messiah as a God, but always as a mere man; and that, if he had impartially examined the sacred prophecies, these then would have instructed him in the truth; and farther, if God should condescend to command him to consult them, in order to perceive how greatly he had erred in his conception, what could the Catholic reply? That God was unjust in condemning him for having taken no means to remove his own blindness, for having confided in his own ignorance, and having believed from interested motives, without examining into what was so essential to his salvation; for having done that which God had not commanded or ordained?

T*

I have not such presumption as to limit the reasons that God might present to the Catholic, in order to force upon him conviction; for the Deity can produce others incomparably more efficacious than my feeble human reason can devise: however, I will only contend that the arguments I have alleged are sufficient to confute the archbishop's presumption, I will not say in the presence of the Divine Being, but certainly before any human tribunal. And if I had to give an account of myself in the manner the preacher describes, and in that character to exculpate myself from no worse charge than that of having professed the law of Moses, I should do it in this form:

"O Lord God, I prostrate myself before thy Divine presence on my knees, to render an account of the religion I professed in my former life, and the reasons that guided me. Lord, I was born of Jewish parents, was instructed in the law of Moses, which I accepted, upon the authority of my teachers, until I attained to years of discretion, when, by reading books of controversy, I was incited to examine, with all the accuracy of which my intellect was capable, the reasons alleged by either party; and having balanced them, unprejudiced by my education, I found that the Divine prophecies that speak of the Messiah had not been fulfilled by any man, until the day of my death. I found, O Lord, in thy holy Law, the assurance, that if our dispersion extended from one end of the world to the other, that we should again be gathered together, and be conducted into the land of promise, where Thou wilt require the observance of thy Divine precepts. How could I change to another religion that destroys and annihilates thy most holy word, that opposes thy Divine commandment, that thyself promulgatedst from Mount Sinai, solely because there are some men who explain certain of the prophecies allegorically, and apply them to a person whom they call thy son, and who have recourse to the figurative sense, because they feel themselves refuted by the literal meaning?

"How could we abandon thy Divine word, that we have heard from thy most holy mouth, for expositions and allegories of men who do not agree among themselves, who contradict and oppose the truth received from thy faithful servant Moses, from thy holy prophets, and from a long succession of sages and learned men; who, through so many ages, have written conformably with that same received truth, which in all their writings they confirm, and have exhorted us to the rigid observance of thy Divine word? These I took for my guide; and believing I was serving and worshipping Thee in the best form and manner that was possible, I connected myself closely with that religion, which I believed to be the only one revealed, and which I recognised for thy true and eternal word. I have lived a Jew, and died a Jew, and in so doing believe I have served Thee as Thou hast commanded, and am now before thy Divine mercy, that Thou mayest order to be done unto me as shall seem good in thy sight, and with the humble persuasion that I have acted in obedience to thy commandments."

And after sentence has been passed on me according to His will, I shall then discover whether judgment is given in heaven accompanied by the same forms as on earth; for, to confess the truth, I am not so well informed on the subject as the good archbishop, nor have I the arrogance to ascribe injustice to God, or to speak of Him with the same freedom; for there is no mocking with "the Divine Majesty." Job says, chapter xiii. verse 9: "It is good that He search you out; for as one man mocketh another, so do you mock Him." Nor shall we ever presume to treat His name with presumption and irreverence, even by way of hypothesis. This is taught me by my holy religion, as Moses says in Deuteronomy, chapter x. verses 20, 21: "Thou shalt fear the Lord thy God; Him shalt thou serve, and to Him shalt thou cleave, and swear by His name. He is thy praise, and He is thy God, that hath done for thee these great and terrible things, which thine eyes have seen."

May He be pleased in His Divine mercy to unveil the eyes of all nations; so that we may all worship Him alike, uniting, in the same mind, to call upon His most holy name with one voice, according to the assurance given us by the prophet Zephaniah, chapter iii. verse 9: "For then will I diffuse among the people a pure language, that they may invoke the name of the Lord, and serve Him with one accord."

THE END.

www.ingramcontent.com/pod-product-compliance
Lightning Source LLC
Chambersburg PA
CBHW021802230426
43669CB00008B/610